FOREWORD BY EDWARD FARRELL

AS BREAD THAT IS BROKEN

by

Peter G. van Breemen, S.J.

DIMENSION BOOKS
Denville, New Jersey

Published by Dimension Books, Inc.
Denville, New Jersey

Imprimatur: Joannes van Deenen, S.J.
Provincial of the Dutch Province
The Hague, Holland, Sept. 12, 1973

*Dedicated to my brothers,
the Dutch Jesuits in renewal*

The parable in Chapter 9 is adapted from a story by A. F.
Wyers published in "De Bazuin" in Holland, August 15,
1959. Used with permission.

TABLE OF CONTENTS

ACKNOWLEDGMENTS

This book has a long history and many people have played a role in the growth of its various chapters. Numerous priests, nuns, laymen and laywomen in three continents have helped through their inspiration and their response; not a few among them have urged and encouraged me to arrange this publication. I want to name two Dutch Jesuits. In the beginning Fr. Jac. de Rooy guided me in breaking the bread of Scripture to make it really accessible as true nourishment; he did so by sharing generously with me his considerable experience. Later Fr. William A. M. Peters proved himself a true teacher; he did so not only through his competence, knowledge and scholarship but also through his concern and encouragement. Without these two men this book would never have been written.

The actual writing and editing of the text was done by Sr. Margaret Hill, O.S.U. With perseverance and great faith in the relevance of the message she devoted herself to all the labor entailed in writing the book. I am very grateful to her for all the work she did and for the way she did it. The title *As Bread that is Broken* is her suggestion. Sr. M. Petronilla, S.M., was a staunch and acute ally in correcting the grammar of the text. Sr. M. Rosina, S.M. graciously created the hospitable atmosphere which was conducive to the actual writing.

FOREWORD

Father Peter van Breemen has a doctoral degree in atomic physics—which is to say that he is a man of our contemporary world of science and technology. He is a Dutch Jesuit—which is to say that he is a man honed in the contemporary church. Most of all, he is a man of deep prayer which is to say "if you read his words, you will have some idea of the depths that he sees in the mystery of Christ" (Eph 3:4).

Gospel means Good News, for those who know how to see and hear, those who believe, Jesus will always be new and he will always be good, attractive, compelling. What van Breemen writes is new and good with the eternal freshness of the daily bread of the Gospel Eucharist.

He writes in depth with a bold simplicity. About God he writes, "He has never revealed Himself except in terms of love. God cannot love but totally, 100%. He cannot love me with anything less of love than that with which He loves His own Son. I cannot lose the love of God because it is not based on any achievement of mine. I don't have to save myself, He will do it!" About man, he writes, "The love, the acceptance of other persons makes me into the unique person I am meant to be. . .when I am not accepted, I cannot come to fulfillment. Not to accept anything from a person is tantamount to killing him, making him sterile. He can't do anything." About prayer, he writes, "Prayer cannot be a means to an end. Prayer

7

is the *last* word—there is no word beyond prayer. . .
Prayer is not efficient, it doesn't bring about anything—it's the stillpoint, the axis around which everything rotates."

This is a dangerous book. Read with faith and openness, it will compel you to follow Him more totally or "to go away sad" (Mk 10:22).

Edward Farrell

One

THE COURAGE TO ACCEPT ACCEPTANCE

There is a basic principle in theology which states that faith or Scripture contains the answer to the deepest questions of the human heart. Faith is about life, my life. Faith is like x-raying my human existence. It helps me to live better, to be more human, to be more integrated. Faith is to discover that there is only a oneness: God is the deepest Ground of my being.

The Question

One of the deepest needs of the human heart is the need to be appreciated. Every human being wants to be valued. This is not to say that everybody wants to be told by others how wonderful he is. No doubt there is that desire, too, but that is not fundamental. We could say that every human being wants to be loved. But even this admits of ambiguity. There are as many varieties of love as there are species of flowers. For some people, love is something passionate; for others, it is something romantic; for others, love is something merely sexual. There is, however, a deeper love, a love of acceptance. Every human being craves to be accepted, accepted for what he is. Nothing in human life has such a lasting and fatal effect as the experience of not being completely accepted. When I am not accepted, then something in me is broken. A baby who is not welcome is ruined at the roots of his existence. A student who does not feel accepted by his teacher will not learn. A man who does not feel accepted by his colleagues on the job will suffer from ulcers, and be a nuisance at home. Many of the life histories of prisoners reveal that somewhere along the way they went astray because there was no one who really accepted them. Likewise, when a religious does not feel accepted by her community, she cannot be happy. A life without acceptance is a life in which a most basic human need goes unfulfilled.

Acceptance means that the people with whom I live give me a feeling of self-respect, a feeling that I am worthwhile. They are happy that I am who I am. Acceptance means that I am welcome to be myself. Acceptance means that though there is need for growth, I am not forced. I do not have to be the person I am not! Neither am I locked in by my past or present. Rather I am given room to unfold, to outgrow the mistakes of the past. In a way we can say that acceptance is an unveiling. Every one of us is born with many potentialities. But unless they are drawn out by the warm touch of another's acceptance, they will remain dormant. Acceptance liberates everything that is in me. Only when I am loved in that deep sense of complete acceptance can I become myself. The love, the acceptance of other persons, makes me the unique person that I am meant to be. When a person is appreciated for what he *does,* he is not unique; someone else can do the same work perhaps even better than he. But when a person is loved for what he *is,* then he becomes a unique and irreplaceable personality. So indeed, I need that acceptance in order to be myself. When I am not accepted, I am a nobody. I cannot come to fulfillment. An accepted person is a happy person because he is opened up, because he can grow.

To accept a person does not mean that I deny his defects, that I gloss over them or try to explain them away. Neither does acceptance mean to say that everything the person does is beautiful and fine. Just the opposite is true. When I deny the defects of the person, then I certainly do not accept him. I have not touched the depth of that person. Only when I accept a person can I truly face his defects.

To express it in a negative way: acceptance means that I never give a person the feeling that he doesn't count. Not to expect anything from a person is tantamount to killing him, making him sterile. He cannot do anything. It is said that children with rickets scratch lime from the walls. People who are not accepted scratch acceptance from the walls. And what are the symptoms?

- boasting: in a subtle or obvious way they provide themselves with the praise they want so badly.
- rigidity: a lack of acceptance causes a lack of security on the path of life and, a fortiori, lack of courage to risk one step to either side of the path.
- inferiority complex: this simply defines the above conditions.
- masturbation or any other superficial joy: deep down there is so much lacking that they endeavor to get whatever they can out of life in an easy way.

11

— the desire to assert themselves, the frightful power to impose themselves, the excessive need for attention, the tendency to feel threatened, to exaggerate, to gossip, to suspect others: these are other symptoms of lack of acceptance.

The really balanced person does not have to indulge in these measures. Erik Erikson in his book, *Young Man Luther,* writes:

> In (his) first relationship man learns something which most individuals who survive and remain sane can take for granted most of the time. Only psychiatrists, priests and born philosophers know how sorely that something can be missed. I have called his early treasure "basic trust;' it is the first psychosocial trait and the fundament of all others. Basic trust in mutuality is that original 'optimism' that assumption that 'somebody is there,' without which we cannot live. In situations in which such basic trust cannot develop in early infancy because of a defect in the child or in the maternal environment, children die mentally. They do not respond or learn; they do not assimilate their food and fail to defend themselves against infection, and often they die physically as well as mentally.[1]

The Answer

I am accepted by God as I am—*as I am,* and not as I should be. To proclaim the latter is an empty message because I never am as I should be. I know that in reality I do not walk a straight path. There are many curves, many wrong decisions which in the course of life have brought me to where I am now and Scripture tells me that "the place on which you stand is holy ground" (Ex 3:5). God knows my name: "See

I have branded you on the palms of my hands"
(Is 49:16). God can never look at his hand without
seeing my name. And my name—that's *me!* He
guarantees that I can be myself. St. Augustine says,
"A friend is someone who knows everything about
you and still accepts you." That is the dream we all
share: that one day I may meet the person to whom
I can really talk, who understands me and the words I
say—who can listen and even hear what is left unsaid,
and then really accepts me. God is the fulfillment of
this dream. He loves me with my ideals and disappointments, my sacrifices and my joys, my successes
and my failures. God is himself the deepest Ground of
my being. It is one thing to know I am accepted and
quite another thing to realize it. It is not enough to
have but just once touched the love of God. There is
more required to build one's life on God's love. It
takes a long time to believe that I am accepted by God
as I am.

How often have we been told that it is important
that we love God. And this is true. But is it far more
important that God loves us! Our love for God is
secondary. God's love for us is first: "This is the love
I mean: not our love for God, but God's love for us"
(1 John 4:10). This is the foundation. Karl Rahner
once made the remark that we live in a time when
there is much interest in Church politics (e.g. the pill,
the reform of the curia, celibate priesthood). This
may be the sign of a deep faith. It can also be the
sign of a lack of faith. The basic faith is that I know
myself to be accepted by God: "We ourselves have
known and put our faith in God's love towards ourselves" (1 John 4:16). This is the content of our

faith—"God's love towards ourselves." The whole Apostles' Creed is nothing but a statement twelve times over of belief in this very love which God has for us.

On the night before he died, Jesus prayed to the Father: "that you love them as you loved me. . .so that your love for me may live in them" (John 17: 23, 26. NAB). It seems incredible that God loves us just as much as he loves his Son, Jesus Christ. Yet that is exactly what Scripture says. We human beings are divided in many ways: 1) in time—For us, one minute comes after the other and our time is spread out. It is not so with God. God lives always in one ever present *now*. There is no division. Eternity means that the whole of time is condensed in this one moment which lasts forever; 2) in space—We have certain limited extensions. It is not so with God. God is completely one; 3) in love—We are divided in our love. We like a person very much (90%) or in an ordinary way (50%) or very little (20%). God does not measure love. God cannot but love totally—100%. If we think God is a person who can divide his love, then we are thinking not of God but of ourselves. God is perfectly one, the perfect unity. We *have* love, but God *is* love. His love is not an activity. It is his whole self. If we but grasp some idea of this, we understand that God could not possibly give 100% of his love to his Son and then 70% to us. He would not be God if he could do that. When we read the dialogues of St. Catherine of Siena, we get the impression that God has nothing to do but simply occupy himself with Catherine. And that is right. The undivided attention of God is with her and with each of us.

14

Tillich defines faith as "the courage to accept acceptance" and he means acceptance by God. We may think that such faith does not demand much courage. On the contrary, it may sound sweet and easy. But courage is required and very often it is courage that is lacking. Why is it courageous to accept acceptance? Firstly, when things happen to us which disappoint us, we are inclined to complain "How can God permit this?" We begin to doubt the love of God. It takes courage to believe in God's acceptance no matter what happens to us. Such an act of faith goes beyond my personal experience. Faith is then an interpretation of life which I accept. Secondly, God's love is infinite. We can never grasp it, never get hold of it, much less control it. The only thing we can do is jump into its bottomless depth. And we do not like to jump. We are afraid to let go. The Swedish convert Sven Stolpe says that faith means to climb a very high ladder, and there while standing on the very top of the ladder, to hear a voice which says, "Jump, and I'll catch you." The one who jumps—he is the man of faith. It is courageous to jump. And there is the third reason which is more subtle but nonetheless real. It is fairly easy to believe in God's love in general but it is very difficult to believe in God's love for me personally. Why me? There are very few people who can really accept themselves, accept acceptance. Indeed, it is rare to meet a person who can cope with the problem "Why me?" Self-acceptance can never be based on my own self, my own qualities. Such a foundation would collapse. Self-acceptance is an act of faith. When God loves me, I must accept myself as well. I cannot be more demanding than God, can I?

Two

THE BEYOND IN OUR MIDST (Psalm 139)

Yahweh, you examine me and you know me,
you know if I am standing or sitting,
you read my thoughts from far away,
whether I walk or lie down, you are watching,
you know every detail of my conduct.

The word is not even on my tongue,
Yahweh, before you know all about it;
close behind and close in front you fence me round,
shielding me with your hand.
Such knowledge is beyond my understanding,
a height to which my mind cannot attain. (v 1-6)

Yahweh really knows me. What does this mean?
When we talk about knowing another person, it is
very often a superficial knowledge. We tend to box
people into categories: he is conservative or liberal; he
is profound or shallow; he is frustrated and bitter or
joyous and full of hope. After having attached enough
labels to the person we glibly say we know everything about him. In fact, we haven't touched the
heart of the person. The psalmist says that God really
knows me as I am, without labels, without categories.
The New Catechism expresses it well: "After all, my
parents could not have wanted 'me.' At best, they
wanted 'a boy' or 'a girl.' Only God wanted 'me.' "[1]
The word "name" in the Hebrew language means that
which makes a person unique. When the Hebrew

claims to know the name of a person, in effect he is saying, "I know this person as a husband knows his wife." We can never know the name of a person unless we really love him. And the fact that God knows my name implies that he loves me:

> Do not be afraid, for I have redeemed you;
> I have called you by your name, you are mine.
> Because you are precious in my eyes
> because you are honoured and I love you (Is 43:2,4).

There are more than three billion people in this world and yet no two of them are identical. There is no mass production with God. Though every person is different, God can put himself in each one without repeating himself. That is the richness of God. Every human being is a prototype—the first and last of a series. God is involved in each of us. He has set himself in the hearts of each one of us. St. Augustine exclaims:

> Late have I loved You, O beauty so ancient and so new! Late have I loved You. Behold You were ever within me, and I abroad, seeking You there. I. . .rushed madly about in the midst of forms beautiful which You had made. You were ever with me, but I was not with You. The very things which had not been, unless they were in You, kept me from You. You called me by name, You cried aloud to me, and Your voice pierced my deafness.[2]

He had looked everywhere for God and God was so close—in the midst of his own heart. St. Paul tells us, "Yet in fact he is not far from any of us, since it is in him we live, and move, and exist" (Acts 17:27-28). That I can be myself is due to God, for he is the source of my being. When I run away or break faith with him, I am no longer me: "Far away from you life is not life. To break faith with you is to be no one"[3]. From whom or what do I run? The problem is not God—"God is closer to me than I am to myself" (St. Augustine)—nor is the tension between God and myself. The cleavage is within me. I am inclined to consider God as a threat, as someone who has set out to de-plume or strip me. But these are false concepts. God is the source of life. He wants me to live and to grow and to come to fulfillment. The threat is me-myself. Often I betray myself. Like St. Paul "I fail to carry out the things I want to do, and I find myself doing the very things I hate" (Rom 7:15). In all these moments God is always on the side of my true self but *I* am not! He is faithful. He is closer to me than I am to myself. Bonhoeffer calls God "the Beyond in our midst"[4]. I can never fathom the mystery of my own personality: "(That's) the paradoxical character of every prayer, of speaking to somebody to whom you cannot speak because he is not 'somebody,' of asking somebody of whom you cannot ask anything because he gives or gives not before you ask, of saying 'Thou' to somebody who is nearer to the I than the I is to itself"[5]. God is more immanent in me than I am in myself. And that "more," that surplus of immanence, is his transcendence. That he is more faithful, that he is closer to me than I am to myself is the divine, the transcendence of God. It proves that he is greater than I. I must adore him. Rather than a threat he is the one guarantee that I can be myself.

Where could I go to escape your spirit?
Where could I flee from your presence?
If I climb the heavens, you are there,
there, too, if I lie in Sheol.

If I flew to the point of sunrise,
or westward across the sea,
your hand would still be guiding me,
your right hand holding me.

If I asked darkness to cover me,
and light to become night around me,
that darkness would not be dark to you,
night would be as light as day (v 7-12).

We cannot hide or run away from God. If "I take the wings of the dawn" (v. 9 NAB), God is still there. Sometimes the presence of God is expressed as something frightening, for instance, in the Book of Job: "What is man that you should make so much of him, subjecting him to your scrutiny, that morning after morning you should examine him and at every instant test him? Will you never take your eyes off me long enough for me to swallow my spittle?" (Job 7:17-19). Job feels watched by God all the time and this upsets him. This describes a period of desolation and confusion in Job's life. In the latter part of the book he returns to his true faith and consolation. The psalmist speaks about God as he really is. That the presence of God is all-embracing does not scare him. It makes him secure: "Wherever I go God is there." This psalm was frequently used in catechetics as a threatening measure. The image of God is symbolized in the ever-watchful eye with the warning finger in front of it. Such a distortion and at what

20

price! Sartre writes in his autobiography, *Les Mots,* of a boyhood experience which bore in seed incalculable consequences. In the midst of an innocent prank he suddenly realized "God sees me." This so frightened him that at the very same moment he made a deliberate choice. He cursed God. In later years he admitted that without this misunderstanding he and God could have gotten along all right. God was used as a stop-gap. Where the education fell short, where parents and teachers could not reach the boy, God was used as a prolongation of education. That is unbiblical, and we see the disastrous results in a man like Sartre. The true God is the source of life, and when the presence of God is expressed as all-embracing, it is meant to be a source of joy. We feel secure because no matter what we do the hand of God has hold of us. That's the way Jesus lived his life. He saw the Father everywhere not as an overseer but as Father—one who loves and provides for his needs:

> That is why I am telling you not to worry about your life and what you are to eat, nor about your body and how you are to clothe it. Surely life means more than food, and the body more than clothing. Look at the birds in the sky. They do not sow or reap or gather into barns; yet your heavenly Father feeds them. Are you not worth much more than they are? Can any of you, for all his worrying, add one single cubit to his span of life? And why worry about clothing? Think of the flowers growing in the fields; they never have to work or spin; yet I assure you that not even Solomon in all his regalia was robed like one of these. Now if that is how God clothes the grass in the field which is there today and thrown into the furnace tomorrow, will he not much more look after you, you men of little faith? (Matt 6:25-31).

The presence of God removes the presence of worries in my life. It doesn't frighten me, but it gives me peace, that safe feeling which goes with true faith.

> It was you who created my inmost self,
> and put me together in my mother's womb;
> for all these mysteries I thank you:
> for the wonder of myself, for the wonder of your works.
>
> You know me through and through,
> from having watched my bones take shape
> when I was being formed in secret,
> knitted together in the limbo of the womb.
>
> You had scrutinised my every action,
> all were recorded in your book,
> my days listed and determined,
> even before the first of them occurred.
>
> God, how hard it is to grasp your thoughts!
> How impossible to count them!
> I could no more count them than I could the sand,
> and suppose I could, you would still be with me (v. 13-18).

The providential care of God is strikingly realized in the miracle of every birth. Each newborn infant demonstrates the tremendous care and attention which God has for each of us. "He put me together" the psalmist exclaims! That I am who I am is due to God. His knowledge is creative. God does not know me because I am, but I am because he knows me. In terms of love (which in God is identical with knowledge) St. Augustine expresses this same truth: "By loving us, God makes us lovable." All of this loving and creative knowledge is a present reality. God knows and loves right now—this very moment. God as the deepest Ground of my being is not a static reality, something dead but rather a dynamic and an ever life-giving activity. This is the mystery I carry within myself. This is the wonder of myself! Scripture does not disregard the worth of myself. On the contrary there is a tremendous esteem for the dignity of man in the Christian revelation. Each of us can join Mary when she sings: "the Almighty has done great things for me" (Lk 1:49). It is good to praise God for what he has accomplished in me. In this prayer of praise my relationship with God is deepened and a sense for the mystery (the "musterion" as the early Church called it) grows. Such an attitude of faith will little by little shape my outlook and my behavior. A prayer life which neglects this sense of wonder becomes more easily stifled and tasteless than the biblical approach of the psalmist: "Bless Yahweh my soul and remember all his kindnesses" (Ps 103:2). The true esteem of man for himself implies the recognition of a dependence on God: the great things *have been done* to me. The very real dignity of my being myself is a dignity which has been received. This is not to make it less valuable. To be sure this awareness of the divine origin makes it all the more precious and reliable. There is a deep peace in this dependence which the world could never give.

> God, If only you would kill the wicked!
> Men of blood, away from me!
> They talk blasphemously about you,
> regard your thoughts as nothing.
>
> Yahweh, do I not hate those who hate you,
> and loathe those who defy you?
> I hate them with a total hatred,
> I regard them as my own enemies.

> God, examine me and know my heart,
> probe me and know my thoughts;
> make sure I do not follow pernicious ways,
> and guide me in the way that is everlasting (v. 19-24).

There is a danger of a false autonomy, of cutting myself off from my roots. Something in each of us rebels against the divine mystery by promising "You will be like gods" (Gen. 3:5). Though God is closer to me than my own self, there is still the perilous possibility of running away from God at the cost of running away from my true self. In the first part of the psalm I relished the truth that God goes with me on all my ways and paths. Now I have to admit that often for all practical purposes I deny this. Earlier I sang with the psalmist of God's wondrous knowledge of my thoughts and deeds and now I realize that he knows, too, the gap that exists between the two. Unconsciously, perhaps, but very really I am my own god not so much in theory as in practice. For as soon as God is no longer the all-important one in my life, he becomes unimportant. To give God the second place would mean to give him no place at all. I am tempted to serve two lords and even to compromise God's position in my life with someone or something else. This is enough to deny him. Idols are not a phenomena of a past era and a primitive culture. We also have idols not of carved wood but in the form of the "in" thing which is just as compelling and evocative. It is not for nothing that John ends his first letter which reads so eloquently of God's love for us and our love for each other: "Children, be on your guard against false gods" (1 Jn 5:21). Idolatry causes sterility and suffering to myself and to others. It is a basic untruthfulness. It is a denial of that infinite depth my life contains. And while I can never fully comprehend the mystery which is my life, through the gift of revelation I accept "the Beyond in our midst." At the end of this magnificent psalm, the psalmist says he is afraid—not afraid of God but afraid of himself and of the possibility which he discovers in himself to ruin the mystery of God in himself and in this world. Humbly and confidently he prays: "Make sure I do not follow pernicious ways, and guide me in the way that is everlasting."

Three

FREE IN TRUTH

"If you make my word your home you
will indeed be my disciples, you will learn
the truth and the truth will make you
free."

John 8:31-32

The word "emeth" is a Hebrew word which until
recently was considered synonymous with the Latin
word "veritas" (truth) and is now translated "fidelitas"
(fidelity). It communicates a knowledge of God. It is
for the Hebrew an existential word. His life, his whole
existence is rooted in the fidelity of Yahweh. He can
trust Yahweh. Yahweh will never let him down. That's
"emeth." To Westerners, truth is something intellectual. Truth means that the idea and the word corre-
spond to reality. This is less profound than the eastern
meaning of the word. John in his Gospel uses the
word many times, e.g., "the truth will make you
free" (Jn 8:32). We miss the whole point if we
interpret truth in this context as meaning intellectual
truth. The truth John speaks of is this: the reliability
of God's love. When I really know that I can trust
Yahweh, that he still accepts me even though I have
sinned— then I am a free person. "Emeth" is the noun,
and the corresponding verb is "aman"—to confirm.
Our "amen" stems from this same verb. God says

27

"amen" to my existence, and he will not go back on his word.

I really do matter to God. He cares for me with all that he is. The most genuine experience of God in mankind points to this unshakeable reality. He has never revealed himself except in terms of love. Once the Chosen People learned this "emeth" of Yahweh, they never forgot it. Though they broke the Covenant, not once but many times, they were always sure of that "emeth." They always knew they could return to Yahweh. He would be there waiting for them. The fullness of this "emeth" has come through Jesus Christ (Jn 1:14,17), the new and everlasting Covenant. St. Paul summarizes beautifully what this "emeth" means: "We may be unfaithful, but he is always faithful, for he cannot disown his own self" (2 Tim 2:13).

This truth in the biblical sense will make men free. The best example of this is the life of Christ. He was a free man—open to everybody. He wasn't bound by rigid laws. He was available to every human person and rejected no one. How did he manage to be so free, so available, so accepting? What was his secret? When Christ speaks—and he speaks through every page of the Gospel—he gives away his secret. He talks about his Father who is the center of his life. He lives in the favor of his Father: "The Father and I are one" (Jn 10:30) and that makes him free indeed. There is no self-concern in Christ, no worry. His heart has found perfect peace through his abandonment to the will of the Father. This is his food (Jn 4:34). It means everything to him.

28

When I do not feel completely accepted, I find ways to assert myself: 1) I become adamant on certain principles. I cannot yield for fear of losing something of my own personality. If, instead, I were to live on God's acceptance I would have no need to assert myself. God has made me worthwhile. I know this in faith, and that is sufficient. 2) I spend my energies not just for the kingdom of God, for the apostolate, but also to build up my own image. How many tensions arise from this! When I really believe in the personal love of God for me, then I am relieved of that part of my work which is nothing but self-assertion. God's love for me is not based on my work. God's love for me is based on nothing: "If Yahweh set his heart on you and chose you, it was not because you outnumbered other peoples: you were the least of all peoples. It was for love of you and to keep the oath he swore to your fathers that Yahweh brought you out with his mighty hand and redeemed you from slavery, from the power of Pharaoh, king of Egypt" (Deut 7:7-9).

God loved me even before I existed. St. Augustine says, "You created me because you loved me." God doesn't love me for what I am, but I am because God loves me. When the love of God is based on nothing, it cannot be destroyed. I can never lose it because it is not due to any achievement of mine. No matter how I behave, that love will remain: "Love consists in this: not that we have loved God but he has loved us" (1 Jn 4:10 NAB). The love of God is a free gift. It gives me freedom, peace and happiness.

As soon as the love of God is no longer the basis, the center of my life, then I become enslaved. I have to cling to something or somebody in order to save myself. When God is the Ultimate Concern in my life, I do not have to save myself. He will do it. In the day-to-day realities I risk losing this freedom. There is a danger that, eventually, secondary values become absolute and thus lose their relationship to the Ultimate Concern. The real problem underlying the confusion is simply that I who possess infinite depth—God is the deepest Ground of my being—identify myself with something limited, something small. I lose not only my freedom but my humanness as well.

There are two types of freedom: the freedom which admits of no external forces in my life—no boss, no superior, no commitments (the limit of this is the spinster!)—and an inner freedom which is capable of surrender, of not being bound by my own likes and caprices. Some "apostles of freedom" are not truly free. The so-called freedom they shout and sing about turns out sometimes to be their personal addictions, *their* ultimate concern. St. Paul reminds us: "My brothers, you were called, as you know, to liberty; but be careful, or this liberty will provide an opening for self-indulgence" (Gal 5:13).

We find in the Gospel an example of persons who are not free at all—the pharisee. He is the counterpart of that freedom which Christ embodies. The most obvious thing we can say about the pharisee is that he is a hypocrite:

Alas for you, scribes and Pharisees, you hypocrites! You who are like whitewashed tombs that look handsome on the outside, but inside are full of dead men's bones and every kind of corruption. In the same way you appear to people from the outside like good honest men, but inside you are full of hypocrisy and lawlessness (Matt 23:27-28).

The pharisee is self-complacent. He is convinced of his own righteousness: "The Pharisee stood there and said this prayer to himself, 'I thank you, God, that I am not grasping, unjust, adulterous like the rest of mankind, and particularly that I am not like this tax collector here' " (Lk 18:11). The opinion of other people is very important to the pharisee: "Everything they do is done to attract attention, like wearing broader phylacteries and longer tassels, like wanting to take the place of honour at banquets and the front seats in the synagogues, being greeted obsequiously in the market squares and having people call them Rabbi" (Matt 23:5-7). The pharisee is very concerned about his own image and will even use prayer to improve it: "And when you pray, do not imitate the hyprocrites: they love to say their prayers standing up in the synagogues and at the street corners for people to see them" (Matt 6:5). He is convinced that, in the kingdom of Yahweh, he has a very important place. It is too bad that the rest of mankind cannot equal him.

That the pharisee fulfills the law is to his credit. But he believes that by keeping the law he saves and justifies himself, and this is his mistake. The pharisee is the man who kills himself in order to observe the law. The law means everything to him. He is conscientious in observing it in every detail. He fasts twice a week; he pays his tithe of mint and dill and cummin. But the emphasis is solely on himself who accomplishes all these things. What is lacking is surrender, abandonment. And he doesn't dare to surrender.

Why? It is the pharisee's idea of God which keeps him locked in. God is a very severe judge, a most cruel critic who is very careful to find fault with man. When he has found fault, he is glad, and he punishes man for it. The whole purpose of the pharisee's life is to live in such a way that he makes no mistake at all. At the end of his life he can show God a perfect slate, and God will have to accept it. His real trouble is that he doesn't believe in any love of God. When we understand the psychology of the pharisee, then the subsequent stages become obvious. When God is cruel, when there is no mercy in God, then the pharisee must keep the law. He must make himself safe. When he does commit a fault, he must repress it because every mistake is fatal. His whole life would be lost. What appears to be hypocrisy is actually a sign that the pharisee cannot accept himself. He needs to tell himself how wonderful he is and he needs to hear this from others because deep inside he is very insecure. There is that fear of God, that terror. He is frightened, but he hides his fear behind a facade of self-complacency. Basically that, too, shows a lack of faith, of feeling accepted.

We can approach this same reality from another angle. When God made a covenant with the Chosen People, they knew themselves loved by Yahweh—they were the apple of his eye! They had but one desire: "How can we please Yahweh." The law explained to the Chosen People what was pleasing to God, and they were happy to receive it (the whole long Psalm 119). It was experienced not as a strain but as a joy: "Listen, Israel: Yahweh, our God, is the one Yahweh. You shall love Yahweh your God with all your heart, with

32

all your soul, with all your strength" (Deut 6:5). Originally, then, the covenant of God's preferential love was basic, and the law was the response of the people to that covenant. As time went on, however, the covenant lost its significance for their lives. To be chosen by God didn't mean much any more. The wholehearted response in joy was gone. The law, however, remained but it had become an obligation, a harness. The law was experienced as a burden and a very heavy one, too. Whereas in the past when the spirituality of the covenant was alive the people felt safe in the shadow of God's love, now in the pharisaic times as the Old Testament deteriorated, the Chosen Ones felt safe in the shadow of the law. The law served as an escape. The law became a shackler. The letter of the law which Christ attacked so vehemently was typical of the pharisee. He saw only the law. But the law has no raison d'être when we do not believe in the covenant of God's love.

The pharisee, then, keeps the law and thinks that because of this he is agreeable to God. God's acceptance is secondary for the pharisee whereas, for Christ, it is exactly the opposite: being agreeable to God comes first. Suppose a child has never experienced any love from his parents, and he sees other children whose parents shower them with affection. The child becomes jealous. He thinks, "I want to be loved, too. I've never experienced it, but I'm going to deserve the love of my parents, to evoke it by my good behavior." The boy works on behaving perfectly to gain the love of his parents. This is the way of the pharisee. He is behaving in such a manner that he is going to induce God's love. The initiative is his. What a terrible world! What an impossible burden! The whole outlook of the Gospel, however, is that of a child who has never experienced anything but love and who tries to do his best because he is loved. Sometimes he makes mistakes but they cause little harm. They do not endanger the love of his parents. The possibility that his parents may stop loving him never enters his mind. For the pharisee, the emphasis is on his own strength and his own achievements, whereas in the Gospel the emphasis is on God's love. What is primary for the pharisee is his own effort but for the man of faith what comes first is his trust in God's love.

There are many types of phariseeism in our lives, many subtle ways in which we succumb to the "Do It Yourself" kit: we observe the law, the rule, better than others perhaps; we run a well-kept prayer life; we keep up with the latest theology of renewal; we live for others and are always available! In a word, we are in the process of making it! We achieve our own salvation. Now all of these four areas are essential. We have to keep the law: "Do not imagine that I have come to abolish the law or the Prophets. I have come not to abolish but to complete them. I tell you solemnly, till heaven and earth disappear, not one dot, not one little stroke, shall disappear from the law until its purpose is achieved" (Matt 5:17). Christ tells his disciples in a parable of the need to pray continually (Lk 18:1). It is also necessary to read the signs of the times: "Hypocrites, you know how to interpret the face of the earth and the sky. How is it you do not know how to interpret these times?" (Lk 12:56). And we will be judged on love: "And the king will

34

answer, 'I tell you solemnly, in so far as you did this to one of the least of these brothers of mine, you did it to me' " (Matt 24:40). When we finish our works of obedience, prayer, renewal or charity, we must smile. This is what the pharisee cannot do. He cannot smile about his own achievements. His whole eternity is at stake, so he is always dead serious and very tense. He is managing his salvation. The man of faith performs like tasks but when he has completed them he says: "This isn't what really counts. What matters is the love of God." In like manner St. Luke tells us, "When you have done all you have been told to do say 'We are merely servants: we have done no more than our duty' " (Lk 17:10). The basic question is not so much "Is God content with me?" but rather, "Is it enough that God is God and that he loves me? " Faith is to believe that God says "Yes" to me, to my being, that God confirms me. When I really believe this, then I, too, can respond "Yes" to God.

Four

AS BREAD THAT IS BROKEN

Prayer is to be in God's presence with open hands and an open heart. There are many things in my life to which I cling as with a clinched fist—my possessions for sure but the immaterial things as well—the work I do, the position I hold, the friends I have, my ideas, my principles, my image. If I should open my fist, they still remain. Nothing drops out. But my hands are open. And that is what prayer is. After a while, if I am willing to remain long enough with open hands, the Lord will come. He will have a look and roam through my hands to see what I have. He may be surprised—so many things! Then he will look at me and ask:

"Would you mind if I take out this little bit?"

And I answer:

"Of course you may take it out. That's why I am here with open hands."

And perhaps the Lord will look another time at me and ask:

"Would you mind if I put something else in your hands?"

And I answer:

"Of course you may."

That is the heart of prayer. The Lord may take something out, and he may put something in. No one else can do this, but he may. He is the Lord. I have only to open my heart and my hands and just stay there long enough for the Lord to come.

Prayer is not so much a searching. Searching suggests a kind of impatience, an activity. I have to do something. Prayer is a waiting. Waiting places the emphasis on the other person who is coming. I can only wait for this person. To wait is to express my powerlessness, my insufficiency, and that is my attitude towards God. I cannot force God to come. All I can do is wait and be present. To pray means to lose my grip. I am no longer in control when I pray. God is in control. He will come when he thinks it is time to come. Prayer is the courage to listen, to give up my self-determination.

Much is expressed just by waiting. Suppose four of us plan to meet at nine o'clock for an outing. Nine o'clock comes and only three of us show up. We wait for the fourth person—fifteen minutes. . .thirty minutes. . .a whole hour. Our waiting says that this fourth person is very important to us. We cannot do without him. So, too, in simply waiting for God, I admit that God is important to my life. I cannot be without him. Edward Farrell in his book, *Surprised by the Spirit,* tells of asking a hermit (Brother John on Cat Island in the Bahamas) to give him a 'word.' But the hermit gave him no answer. He had no 'word' to pass on. Four or five days later, when Father Farrell was leaving the island, Brother John had this to say: "When you go back and talk with your people, tell them to be patient with God, to wait for Him."[1]

Prayer is waiting. It is this waiting which stamps, shapes my personality. When I am willing to wait, I become different. Prayer makes a person attentive,

38

contemplative. Instead of being manipulative, the prayerful man is receptive in this world. He doesn't grasp, but he caresses; he doesn't bite, but he touches; he doesn't question, but he admires and adores. St. John of the Cross defined his ideal in life "to live in loving, attentive expectancy." This is the right attitude of a man towards God. Bonhoeffer reflects, "If you refuse to be with yourself alone, you are rejecting Christ's call to you."[2] One has to be alone to stand the waiting. One has to wait—not try to run away—but wait with one's whole being.

The heart of prayer is the realization of God's love for me and my response in total surrender to his love. This personal interaction between God and man we know as adoration. It demands the involvement of one's whole being. It is the ultimate act of man. Once a person has become completely adoration, he has reached the utter fulfillment which we call heaven. This will last forever. There is nothing beyond it; it is the very end. Adoration, therefore, can never be used as a means to an end. It is, by its very nature, disinterested. It is not efficient nor does it achieve anything. That is why it is so difficult. Our lives are purposefully planned and meant to produce results. Even our moments of relaxation must achieve something! Prayer is the one big exception. It is the stillpoint, the axis around which all other activities rotate. When that axis is missing, our lives become pointless. But the axis itself serves no useful purpose in the strict sense of the word. As long as I aim at something in my prayer, I am bound to be disappointed. This is one of the major difficulties in the life of prayer; I fail to see the "usefulness" of it at a certain stage and feel tempted, then, to give it up.

Many a sermon has tried to convince us why it is "useful" to pray:
- God hears our prayer of petition.
- Prayer gives a wisdom and insight which can be found nowhere else.
- Prayer brings about a deep peace which the world can neither give nor take away.
- Prayer is a source of strength which pulls us through all the difficulties of our lives.

All these motives to pray are valid but they do not touch the ultimate depth of prayer. They are secondary to the "why" of prayer. Prayer cannot be measured in terms of "usefulness." It can only be understood as a complete surrender without wanting "to get something out of it." The time will come when the secondary reasons for prayer break down, when they no longer convince me enough to want to continue to pray. The time will come when I feel that my prayer is not heard. The time will come when I experience prayer as a total waste of time, when I discover no insights to relish, no feelings of fulfillment. Then I might be tempted to turn my prayer into a half hour of reading or a nature walk. At least I can get something out of that! And the time will come when prayer brings no peace, when it consumes my strength and makes me realize my weakness. How do I resolve these difficulties? What is prayer? Prayer *is* a waste of time. And more than that—it is a waste of *self*. This waste of time is a very real and sorely needed symbol of a far deeper loss and surrender that "happens" in every authentic prayer! "Who loses his soul will find it" is the heart of all true prayer. This is not to say that prayer has no fruitful effects but only that its "usefulness" cannot be the end of prayer. A friendship can offer many "useful" benefits but if they are the sole purpose of the friendship, then there is no friendship at all. In the words of Meister Eckhart, a spiritual writer of the Middle Ages: "To use God is to kill him."

The life of prayer can be explained in three stages. In the first stage the prayer centers on the realization that God is love, that he loves me *as I am* (not as I should be). He knows my name; it is written in the palm of his hand. He loved me first. Prayer is basking in the sun of God's love until it finally penetrates my whole being, until I know it in my heart (heart understood as the center of myself, above and beyond the intelligence, will and emotions; that which makes me myself). Prayer means to be utterly secure in the presence of God. Prayer, therefore, can never be an attempt to make God change his mind: this is a pagan concept. To pray is to surrender to the love of God, to abandon myself and to say whole-heartedly without fear: "Your kingdom come, your will be done."

It is not enough to know that God is love, I cannot live on this. The idea which strikes me so force-ably today all too quickly dims to a pale shadow. God knows I am human. He has made his love tangible, visible in Christ: "Who sees me, sees the Father" (Jn 14:9). Prayer in its second stage, then, is concentrated on the person of Christ. It means that I try to know Christ better, to love and follow him more closely as St. Ignatius states it repeatedly in the *Spiritual*

41

Exercises and as we sing in the similar words of *Godspell:* "Three things I pray: to see you more clearly, love you more dearly, follow you more nearly, day by day." This knowledge will grow into a personal relationship with Christ and eventually mature into the most profound relationship of my life as it was for St. Paul who could write: "I live now not with my own life but with the life of Christ who lives in me" (Gal 2:20) and "Life to me, of course, is Christ" (Phil 1:21). A more recent example of this friendship with Christ is found in the life of Dietrich Bonhoeffer who wrote in a letter of August 21, 1944:

The key to everything is the 'in him.' All that we may rightly expect from God, and ask for, is to be found in Jesus Christ. The God of Jesus Christ has nothing to do with what God, as we imagine him, could do or ought to dò. If we are to learn what God promises, and what he fulfills, we must persevere in quiet meditation on the life, sayings, deeds, sufferings, and death of Jesus. . .In Jesus God has said Yes and Amen to it all, and that Yes and Amen is the firm ground on which we stand. In these turbulent times we repeatedly lose sight of what really makes life worth living. We think that, because this or that person is living, it makes sense for us to live too. But the truth is that if this earth was good enough for the man Jesus Christ, if such a man as Jesus lived, then, and only then, has life a meaning for us. If Jesus had not lived, then our life would be meaningless, in spite of all the other people whom we know and honour and love.3

The third stage of prayer is finding God involved in the whole of reality. Not only in Jesus Christ can I find God but in every person and, in fact, in every thing. Prayer now means to say "Yes" to reality, to have a positive attitude towards life, to confirm what is, not for shallow reasons but because God is the deepest Ground of all being. Prayer means that there is a personal relationship between the deepest Ground of everything that exists—and me. Prayer means that I realize that the deepest Ground has a name, and that I pronounce that name. Only then do I pray in the true sense of the word.

Prayer touches the deepest Ground. It implies waiting—as before any birth—in darkness and expectancy. Since prayer takes place at the root of my life, my whole life is at stake. Prayer can never be a part of my life nor an attempt to bribe God. I can never pray unless I am willing to commit myself completely. Many difficulties in prayer stem from the fact that people really do not want to commit themselves. Yet unless we give ourselves totally, our prayer is not authentic. Prayer can never be a substitute for the real gift of my entire self. Take, for example, my time. Every night at midnight I receive a gift—twenty-four hours. Prayer means that I let go of those twenty-four hours, that I use them in the way that God wants me to use them. When my prayer is sincere, I always say one way or another, "Your will be done." Consequently, I can never claim my own time. Buber explains it well when he says: "prayer is not in time but time in prayer. . .to reverse the relation is to abolish reality."[4] The twenty-four hours are rooted in prayer. And when I am bold enough to pray even for five minutes, those twenty-four hours are no longer mine. Intuitively I feel the struggle. When I pray, I have to make a choice, a very fundamental choice: namely, will God be God of my life or not. I have to give an answer to this question when I pray. When I do not pray, I do not have to make that choice yet. I can postpone the choice until. . .

Prayer transforms me into bread that is broken. It is in the breaking of the bread that I am made available often in ways which remain hidden to me. As bread I am given not once but many times, over and over. Prayer both demands and instills the willingness to accept this mystery as a call to which I respond with my whole being. It is in the breaking of the bread that I realize the paschal mystery of death and resurrection. If I am to live this mystery, then I must pray; otherwise, I will never be able to live it. On the other hand, if I want to pray, I must be open to live this mystery; otherwise, I can never pray.

I must live in such a way that I can pray. Difficulties in prayer are often would-be difficulties. The real difficulty is not so much prayer but the way I live. Sometimes I complain that prayer makes me tense, I cannot pray regularly. This is surely an escape. Prayer doesn't create tension. My way of life simply does not agree with my prayer. When I pray without open hands, when I do not give God complete freedom, when I refuse what I know he is clearly asking of me—then my prayer is dry and empty and desolate. I cannot say "Your will be done." This type of prayer is like playing a game of tennis on a court in which there is a one-foot iron pole somewhere in the middle of my half of the court. With the fear of running into that pole constantly on my mind, I cannot enjoy the match. Instead of being relaxed I become tense and frightened. The whole game is spoiled. I either give up in a short while or I finish the game, not gracefully, but with a dogged determination, an achievement of just not having given up. In somewhat the same way prayer can turn into an achievement, something which I do faithfully every day (like watching TV, eating three meals a day). This prayer is inauthentic. It is an illusion. My life is not at stake. Such a habit of refusal, such blind obstinacy nourishes a deep-seated hypocrisy which gradually penetrates every aspect of my life. Thomas Merton describes this inauthentic prayer as "bogus interiority." It gives a semblance of pious sanctity but in reality it is something achieved and not lived. And, Merton continues, "It is unfortunately all too true that bogus interiority has saved face for pious men and women who were thus preserved from admitting their total nonentity."[5] Worst of all is the harm these people do to others who want to learn to pray. They take away the appeal of prayer—"If that is prayer, I do not want it." They create a tremendous anti-propaganda for prayer. Why? Because their prayer is not authentic. But who can find that out?

Five

TEACH US TO PRAY

"Now once Jesus was in a certain place praying and when he had finished one of his disciples said, 'Lord, teach us to pray' " (Lk 11:1). Jesus told them in a parable of the need to pray continually and never to lose heart (Lk 18:1). There are several theories on prayer making the rounds of today's circle of thought all of which reflect something old and something new. We hear it said that everything is prayer: "I pray all day!" Beautiful as this may sound, there is a danger here that prayer lose its meaning and content. When everything is prayer, then prayer itself is nothing. There are those who say "My work is my prayer." This is an ambiguous statement because in one sense it is true, but in another sense it is false. I cannot pray and then not live up to it. The work I do surely reflects the authenticity of my prayer. But I am fooling myself if I allow my work to replace my prayer or if I find prayer only "useful" insofar as it motivates me to action. Prayer is something real. It has a value which extends far beyond the limits of my vision.

To grasp something of this reality I must dispose myself for it. I must begin to pray. Difficulty in prayer occurs because I do not begin properly. If the borderline between my work and my prayer is thin or has even disappeared, if I maintain that I can pray anywhere and in any circumstances, I will no doubt make a poor beginning of my prayer. I will tend more or less to simply continue to be engrossed in the previous activity, e.g., a telephone call, a letter, a conversation. When I pray I must leave the trivialities of life behind; they do not have a place in my prayer. On the other hand, what really touches my heart should touch my prayer. Prayer has no point, no reality, unless it is firmly rooted in life. Some people have a "praying coat" which they put on when they begin to pray. Then, after an hour or so, they remove the coat and return to reality. This is a nice escape from life but it is not prayer. Why? Because it is not real. When I receive word that someone dear to me is seriously ill, I cannot and should not dismiss this from my prayer. But there are two ways of handling this: I can worry about it and let my imagination run wild, or I can bring it to the level of prayer: "Cast your worries on the Lord" (1 Pet 5:7). I can commend my friend to God. I can trust that God holds him in his hands. Now I can pray about what is important to me and pray in a very real way.

How do I begin to pray? There is a difference between concentration on the object I place before me which concentration requires much will power, and recollectedness ("Sammlung" in German) which is simply "to let go," an immediate oneness or union with the object I contemplate. Concentration is tiring and, therefore, short-lived. Recollectedness requires no strain and can last a long time. I have to begin my prayer with a few minutes of concentration in order to pull myself together, but then I "let go." I identify with the object of my contemplation, e.g., God the

48

Father, Jesus Christ, or any other person from the Gospel. My whole being is tranquil and quiet. God is there. He has been waiting for me.

Maybe I am willing to pray and I pray well, but I have another difficulty. I do not feel that God answers my prayer. This is turning things upside down. God is not the one who is answering.. God is first. I am but a word spoken by God. I am the one who answers:

> You have first loved us, O God, alas. We speak of it in terms of history, as if you have only loved us first but a single time, rather than that without ceasing you have loved us first many times and every day and our whole life through. When we wake up in the morning and turn our soul to you...You are the first...You have loved us first; if I rise at dawn and at the same time turn my soul towards you in prayer, You are there ahead of me; You have loved me first. When I withdraw from the distractions of the day and turn my soul in thought towards You, you are the first and thus forever. And yet we always speak ungratefully as if You have loved us first only once.[1]
>
> Soren Kierkegaard

So I try to make myself still. I try to listen to God. I listen not just to the message I want to hear but, with complete openness, to what God wants to tell me:

> Contemplation is essentially a listening in silence, an expectancy. And yet in a certain sense, we must truly begin to hear God when we have ceased to listen. Because there is a higher kind of listening, which is not a receptivity to a certain kind of message only. The true contemplative is not the one who prepares his mind for a particular message that he wants or expects to hear; but he remains empty because he knows that he can never

expect or anticipate the word that will transform his darkness to light.

This silence is not a kind of 'blacking out' which one does of set purpose, as a conclusion to practical reasoning on the subject, a sort of artificial darkness of one's own making. Such a person is not alone with God, but alone with himself. He is not in the presence of the Transcendent One, but of an idol: his own complacent identity. He becomes immersed and lost in himself, in a state of inert, primitive and infantile narcissism.[2]

Again, some people say that they do not like to pray because they cannot tolerate introspection. However, prayer is not facing myself; it is facing God. To pray means to turn the spotlight on Christ. What *I* should do is gradually revealed to me. It happens to me. I discover it without self-analysis. On the contrary, the desire to examine myself or to see myself grow is a degeneration and a set-back in the life of prayer. Slowly and peacefully, in coming to know Christ, I come to know myself.

What follows is a plausible scheme which may be helpful for growth in prayer. It is not intended to stifle our prayer as a harness but rather to clarify our concepts of prayer so that the experience becomes more lucid and free. The scheme has five levels and, surprisingly, we begin at the top!

1. Prayer begins with the realization that I am loved by God as I am. His love is based on nothing and, therefore, is the most basic and secure fact in my life. I simply let myself be loved by God. This is not so much an activity of mine but a passivity in which I let God's love soak in and permeate my whole being. It is the most restful attitude a person can take and the most fruitful as well. I should remain on this level

as long as I can, neither a longer nor a shorter time. Why not shorter? Because even if I should spend all my time on this level, it would be more valuable than anything I could do! Why not longer than I feel I can? Because I would be forcing myself and that is always wrong. When I sense that I am satisfied, I move on to the next level.

2. My response to God's love is an activity of mine, and in this instance, it is the highest and most intense act of which I am capable; namely, adoration. To adore is to abandon myself completely into the loving hands of God. God may dispose of me—"Your will be done. . ." I can pray this without any tension or apprehension because I am convinced that God is no threat to me, that he is the source of life and fulfillment. This prayer of adoration can be made with or without words, in my own words or in the words of another. Again I stay in this adoration as long as I can without pressure to either shorten or prolong the moment.

3. Next, I refer to a particular episode in Scripture (or of a book which helps me to pray) but in such a way that I try to identify with Christ or with a person with whom Christ is dealing. This means that I contemplate a Gospel event not as an onlooker from the sidelines but as a participant—as one deeply involved. This is not a matter of the imagination which conjures up a vivid scene but a matter of the heart (in the biblical sense) which knows itself related to Christ. It is no longer I who live but it is Christ who lives in me—who speaks in me or touches me or heals me. This can be a very prayerful experience. Again I remain there no longer nor shorter a time than I can.

4. Then comes the prayer of petition. The prayer becomes more and more active as I go down the steps of the scheme. From what I have considered thus far, many petitions will suggest themselves. I may ask to know Christ better, to have greater faith in him, more courage and generosity to follow him, more love for the people who come into my life, or any other grace. Here, again, I can express my prayer in my own words, or in the words of the psalms, or in any other prayer which I find helpful.

5. The last step is meditation in the technical sense of the word. I open Scripture or another book which I want to use for my prayer, and I consider a verse or a passage. This is a kind of intellectual process. It includes thinking, analysis, investigation, the effort to understand what is meant by these words. Hopefully, this thinking will lead me to the prayer of petition or to a renewed identification with Christ, perhaps to a period of adoration or even to a passive abiding in God's love. From the level of meditation in the strict sense I may ascend to higher levels of prayer. Prayer is like a mountain landscape in which I am led by the Spirit to pause at various stages along the way.

To conclude: there is a dictum which relativizes the above scheme—"Pray as you can and don't try to pray as you can't" (Dom Chapman).

Six

YOU ARE THE MAN (2 Sam 11 and 12)

"At the turn of the year, the time when kings go campaigning, David sent Joab and with him his own guards and the whole of Israel. They massacred the Ammonites and laid siege to Rabbah. David however remained in Jerusalem. It happened towards evening when David had risen from his couch and was strolling on the palace roof, that he saw from the roof a woman bathing; the woman was very beautiful" (11:1-2). A warrior has nothing with which to occupy his time. After his nap he paces up and down on the palace roof. There is nothing wrong in this, but the boredom reveals the power of evil which lurks as a kind of fifth column within each of us: "The heart is more devious than any other thing, perverse too: who can pierce its secrets?" (Jer 17:9). Evil is part of ourselves and the slightest provocation is enough to bring it to the surface.

"David made inquiries about this woman and was told, 'Why, that is Bathsheba, Eliam's daughter, the wife of Uriah the Hittite.' Then David sent messengers and had her brought. She came to him, and he slept with her; now she had just purified herself from her courses. She then went home again" (v3-4). We carry our treasures in vessels of clay. Blessed Claude de la Colombiere said, "I feel within myself the possibility of every sin." We, too, bear

53

within ourselves this possibility and it is good to realize it. At least, it should prevent us from being too easily shocked by the evil we see in others. We can seldom locate the moment in which we premeditated, devised some real evil. That rarely happens. It is always a slow process. It originates with a fairly innocent weakness. Here it is sensuous curiosity—a human weakness we all share. But, rather quickly, the evil develops into a full-scale murder: at the end of this story Uriah is killed. This is how evil grows in our lives, too. It begins with a triviality. That is human. But the growth is also human. It takes a certain span of time for evil to be born. And that is precisely what makes it real. Many situations in which we live have an intrinsic logic. What does this mean? When I tell a lie, for example, it may be a little thing. But once I've told one lie, I have to tell one more to remain consistent. Soon I am entangled in a net of lies. I have become a liar. This is what is termed the intrinsic logic of the situation. Another example is divorce. Divorce doesn't just happen. It, too, has a history. It has grown over a period of time. It may begin with a sense of disappointment. Maybe the husband has a fear of getting old and he projects this fear onto his wife. His disappointment makes him moody and he begins to lose interest in his wife. That is not too bad. But again, the situation contains within it an intrinsic logic. Slowly the husband and wife drift apart. He becomes interested in another woman but not seriously: she is only an oasis in a desert of monotony. It is just an innocent game. Gradually the dream of a new beginning becomes real. The two become more and more involved. And, after a while, they realize that they are on a dangerous path, but they keep telling each other "We'll manage. We'll remain within the limits." They are fooling themselves. The intrinsic logic goes further and further. Eventually it ends in divorce. Like everything that lives, evil begins with a seed; then it takes root and grows.

There is a significant difference between the Old and the New Testament in their approach to evil. In the Old Testament it is the law which counts, and the law deals with evil which is visible and tangible: "You have learnt how it was said to our ancestors: you must not kill: and if anyone does kill he must answer for it before the court" (Matt 5:21). Christ, however, deals with the root of evil, the seed, there where no law can penetrate: "But I say to you: anyone who is angry with his brother will answer for it before the court" (Matt 5:22). Again, "You have learnt how it was said: You must not commit adultery" (Matt 5:27). Adultery is classified by law and punishable by death. But Christ says, "If a man looks at a woman lustfully, he has already committed adultery with her in his heart" (Matt 5:28). Repeatedly Christ strikes at the root: "But the things that come out of the mouth come from the heart, and it is these that make a man unclean" (Matt 15:17).

"The woman conceived and sent word to David, 'I am with child' " (v 5). David aims now to repudiate his guilt. He has only one concern: to save face. He is not going to admit his guilt. He becomes increasingly fanatic. A blindness to everything but this concern overcomes him. All the power of the throne is employed towards this one purpose of preserving his honor. For no reason whatever David orders Uriah to

55

take leave from battle. He even requests his presence at court: "When Uriah came into his presence, David asked after Joab and the army and how the war was going. David then said to Uriah, 'Go down to your house and enjoy yourself' " (v 7-8). Uriah, however, is not fooled: "Uriah however slept by the palace door with his master's bodyguard and did not go down to his house" (v 9). David's first attempt fails. The next morning David hears that Uriah did not go home. He calls for Uriah again: "So David asked Uriah, 'Have you not just arrived from a journey? Why do you not go to your home?' But Uriah answered, 'Are not the ark and the men of Israel and Judah lodged in tents; and my master Joab and the bodyguard of my lord, are they not in the open fields? Am I to go to my house, then, and eat and drink and sleep with my wife? As Yahweh lives, and as you yourself live, I will do no such thing' "(v 10b-11). Aware that this second attempt is not succeeding, David orders Uriah to return to battle: "Then David said to Uriah, 'Stay on here today; tomorrow I shall send you back.' So Uriah stayed that day in Jerusalem" (v 12). Meanwhile David makes a third attempt: "The next day David invited him to eat and drink in his presence and made him drunk. In the evening Uriah went out and lay on his couch with his master's bodyguard, but he did not go down to his house" (v 13). Even though Uriah is drunk, he is strong enough to stand by his principles. David then sends Uriah back to the front lines with a message for Joab, the general' "Next morning David wrote a letter to Joab and sent it by Uriah. In the letter he wrote, 'Station Uriah in the thick of the fight and then fall back

56

behind him so that he may be struck down and die.'
Joab, then besieging the town, posted Uriah in a
place where he knew there were fierce fighters. The
men of the town sallied out and engaged Joab; the
army suffered casualties, including some of David's
bodyguard; and Uriah the Hittite was killed too" (v
14-17). David is willing to go to any extreme. And he
believes that by doing this he saves face. But that is
not at all true. From the very first moment Uriah has
suspected. Joab also surmises what is at hand. And
this is normal in the repression of guilt: we think that
people do not notice it, but they do. With the loss of
a battle Joab has to get word to the king, and he does
so in a clever way. Joab instructs the messenger to tell
David of the defeat and then to wait. After David's
outburst of anger, the messenger is to add, "Your
servant Uriah the Hittite has been killed too" (v 21).
The messenger carries out the orders and David reacts
as predicted. As soon as he hears of Uriah's death, he
changes completely: "Then David said to the messenger, 'Say this to Joab, "Do not take the matter to
heart; the sword devours now one and now another.
Storm the town in greater force and overthrow it."
That is the way to encourage him' " (v 25). The
repression of guilt is far worse than the sin David
committed with Bathsheba. If he had confessed,
admitted his guilt, it would not have been too bad.
The real evil started when he tried to repress his guilt.

"Yahweh sent Nathan the prophet to David. He
came to him and said:

'In the same town were two men, one rich and the other
poor. The rich man had flocks and herds in great
abundance; the poor man had nothing but a ewe lamb,

57

one only, a small one he had bought. This he fed, and it grew up with him and his children, eating his bread, drinking from his cup, sleeping on his breast; it was like a daughter to him. When there came a traveler to stay, the rich man refused to take one of his own flock or herd to provide for the wayfarer who had come to him. Instead he took the poor man's lamb and prepared it for his guest.

David's anger flared up against the man. 'As Yahweh lives,' he said to Nathan 'the man who did this deserves to die! He must make fourfold restitution for the lamb, for doing such a thing and showing no compassion' " (12:1-6). David's conscience functions well in regard to others. He sees clearly in the rich man the very fault which is his. Confucius says, "When you see a noble man, try to equal him. When you see an evil man, examine yourself thoroughly." Very often the beam in our own eye is the best magnifying glass for detecting the splinter in the other person's eye. After all, it is the same material! David lives in a precarious peace of conscience by dedicating himself to a world which is outside himself. The behavior of the rich man annoys and upsets him. He even dictates the punishment he should receive. In accusing the other person there is no energy left to face and confess his own guilt. His zeal is an escape. How often this occurs in our life experience. The guilt David points out so vehemently in the rich man is a very real crime which indeed needs to be punished. And yet David's passion for justice veils a basic injustice in himself. The eagerness to reform and the generous dedication to causes of others can indeed hide a subtle repression of personal fear and guilt. Psychiatrists tell us how through activism a person sometimes tries to quench feelings of fear and guilt by making himself available to others in a very liberal way. This attitude can make the person very attractive and only few realize what kind of escape is going on behind this facade. David will admit that he is himself a sinner. But he will not confess this particular sin. He will not say "I killed a man." Sometimes the sins we confess are the innocuous ones. That makes the situation even more dangerous. It is another subtle way of repressing guilt. "Then Nathan said to David, 'You are the man.' " This is the moment of conversion: "The word of God is something alive and active: it cuts like any double-edged sword but more finely' it can slip through the place where the soul is divided from the spirit, or joints from the marrow; it can judge the secret emotions and thoughts" (Heb 4:12). The word of God is addressed to David through another man. He needed someone else to enable him to come to the admission of his guilt: "I have sinned against Yahweh" (v 13). As long as we repress our guilt, we show that we do not feel completely accepted. When we really accept God's acceptance and believe that his acceptance is without limits, then we can express our guilt. The mere fact that we repress our guilt is a sign that we do not fully believe in God's love. And that is the worst point about repression. It indicates a lack of faith, a lack of knowing ourselves to be accepted. Sometimes we meet people who cannot admit their mistakes, cannot say they are sorry. These people are to be pitied for their insecurity. They are very weak people and they suffer greatly:

"All the time I kept silent, my bones were wasting away
   with groans, day in, day out;
day and night your hand
   lay heavy on me;
My heart grew parched as stubble
   in summer drought.

At last I admitted to you I had sinned;
   no longer concealing my guilt,
I said, 'I will go to Yahweh
   and confess my fault.'
And you, you have forgiven the wrong I did,
   have pardoned my sin."   Ps 32:3-5

The right answer is not found in repression but in forgiveness: "Happy the man whose fault is forgiven, whose sin is blotted out" (Ps 32:1). What a blessing for him that his sins do not count anymore with God. The courage to admit "I have sinned" can only be found in faith. And then that very forgiveness reveals a new depth in the love of God, another dimension of the Good News. In the moment of forgiveness the evil we committed is turned into something good. We come to know God better. We experience and realize then that his acceptance is without limits. His love is greater than our guilt. The forgiveness creates a new bond between God and ourselves. That is why the revelation of sin is a work of the Holy Spirit (see Jn 16:8). Only the man who has found the courage to confess his guilt can really accept himself and find that peace which the world cannot give or take away.

Seven

HE IS ALWAYS FAITHFUL

Even a cursory glance at the New Testament reveals the existence of a special relationship between Jesus and sinners. Jesus scandalized many people because of his associations with them, yet he continued to seek them. He had to. His name is Jesus—"because he is the one who is to save his people from their sins" (Matt 1:21).

"While he was at dinner in the house it happened that a number of tax collectors and sinners came to sit at the table with Jesus and his disciples. When the Pharisees saw this, they said to his disciples, 'Why does your master eat with tax collectors and sinners?' When he heard this he replied, 'It is not the healthy who need the doctor, but the sick. Go and learn the meaning of the words: What I want is mercy, not sacrifice. And indeed I did not come to call the virtuous, but sinners' " (Matt 9:10-13). Jesus has little time for the virtuous "for the Son of Man has come to seek out and save what was lost" (Lk 19:10). This is the heart of his mission: he has been sent by the Father to seek sinners. He had not come to denounce middle class habits, to provoke and upset the establishment, to instigate a social revolution or to take sides with the outcasts. In short, his purpose was not to straighten man's relationship with his fellow man. Sometimes his actual mission will include that but it remains secondary. Jesus had but one objective: to straighten man's relationship with God. He came to call sinners.

There is a link between the miracles he worked and the forgiveness of sins: "Seeing their faith, Jesus said to the paralytic, 'My child, your sins are forgiven' " (Mk 2:5). The paralytic had not been brought for that! He wanted to be cured. After expressing the purpose of his mission and proclaiming that this has been accomplished in this man, Jesus adds as a token of forgiveness "Get up, pick up your stretcher and walk" (Mk 2:10). To cure and to forgive were two distinct levels of Jesus' mission. It is a remarkable fact that Jesus healed the sick who were brought to him but he did not go after them. The sinners were much more the object of his concern. With them, he took the initiative to show his genuine acceptance. He befriended the Publicans and prostitutes. He chose one of his apostles from among them. He was seen in their presence. He even had dinner with them. And he made this scandalous conduct the object of his mission, the purpose of his coming. While in many ways Christ was like the prophets, on this point he was different. He received tax collectors and the like:

> In this reversal lies the whole of Christianity. Until Jesus came, the religious impulse was always marked by man's need to escape his guilt, to find a way of overcoming the evil which lives in him and making amends for the contagion which, despite himself, he continually spreads around him. . .But Jesus' answer overturns all questions: instead of saying what one must do and where one must go, it asserts that God comes to forgive, and it offers proof of this: Jesus is now in the midst of sinners, eating and drinking with them.[1]

God goes out of his way, sends his only Son to seek sinners. He makes no distinctions. In his eyes we are all sinners: "As they persisted with their question, he looked up and said, 'If there is one of you who has not sinned, let him be the first to throw a stone at her' "(Jn 8:7).

Before he can cure us we must admit that we are ill. No doctor can ever heal a patient who refuses to admit he is sick. We can be saved only on condition that we confess our need to be saved. God respects our freedom. He does not force himself into our lives and he will not redeem us if we refuse. Who considers himself as just, as virtuous, puts himself outside the sphere of Christ's influence. Where there is no consciousness of sin, Christianity operates in a void. The whole Gospel loses its meaning and purpose: "If we say we have no sin in us, we are deceiving ourselves and refusing to admit the truth;. . .To say that we have never sinned is to call God a liar and to show that his word is not in us" (1 Jn 1:8,10). Christ came not to arouse or agitate the milieu. There was more at stake. Jesus sought to bring about a revolution in the very depth of man—there where he blocks out the love of God. In this revolution Jesus himself takes the initiative: "For this reason I tell you that her sins, her many sins, must have been forgiven her, or she would not have shown such great love" (Lk 7:47). There are two interpretations of this text: Either the woman showed such tremendous love and therefore her sins were forgiven or her sins were forgiven and therefore she showed tremendous love. The first interpretation would be Old Testament. The prophets would do the same. When a sinful woman came, cried and repented, they forgave. In the Gospel the process is reversed. The forgiveness comes first and as a result the woman shows unbounded love. In the process of forgiveness our eyes are opened and we realize the lavishness of God's love. And then we are free to respond. The initiative is God's—God forgives. The fruit is ours—an increase in love, a better understanding of the truth of Yahweh.

Jesus will never belittle sin. But he will forgive: " 'Has no one condemned you?' 'No one, Sir.' she replied. 'Neither do I condemn you,' said Jesus, 'go away and don't sin any more' " (Jn 8:10b-11). That was typical of Christ. He accepted the adulterous woman as she was. There was no condemnation. He called her deed a sin but without offending her. Christ doesn't "speak" us free. He makes us free. His message is not a lecture but a fact, something that happens. The Son of God with the fullness of God in him becomes one of us. He shares in our sinfulness, and the depth of this solidarity achieves reconciliation for those who wish to receive it. To understand something of the mind of Christ we must understand the importance of reconciliation in the New Testament.

In Scripture, and especially in the New Testament, brotherhood is stressed strongly. The love-for-one-another is the commandment which equals the great commandment of loving God with one's whole heart and strength. This Christian brotherhood is not based on ideals of humanity and humanitarianism but solely on the reconciliation which God by himself has accomplished. It is the fruit of God's saving operation. In Christ, the reconciliation of man to God has been established, and consequently, the reconciliation of men among themselves. This reconciliation is the key concept which opens the door to all other biblical concepts such as forgiveness, redemption, salvation, justification, sanctification, peace, charity:[2]

> For anyone who is in Christ, there is a new creation; the old creation has gone, and now the new one is here. It is all God's work. It was God who reconciled us to Himself through Christ and gave us the work of handing on this reconciliation. In other words, God in Christ was reconciling the world to Himself, not holding men's faults against them, and he has entrusted to us the news that they are reconciled. So we are ambassadors for Christ; it is as though God were appealing through us, and the appeal that we make in Christ's name is: be reconciled to God (2 Cor 5:17-20).

Not only is the reconciliation of primary importance for the preaching of the Gospel. The living of the Gospel depends on it as well. For how can we ever manage to love unselfishly, to serve humbly and patiently in spite of frustration if we do not live on God's forgiveness? The Sermon on the Mount presupposes the personal experience of God's forgiveness. Much zealous dedication in the Church does not bear good fruit because it is not founded in reconciliation. Only a person who realizes his own guilt and knows that it is forgiven, can love his enemy. He who underestimates the reality of sin is naive and shallow and will not go far in his service of others. But he who underestimates the reality of forgiveness traps himself in the vicious circle of frustration and aggression and will soon be rutted in his efforts to create a better world. Brotherhood based on either premise alone is no longer evangelical. The message of reconciliation enables man to face everything that is human without getting despondent or depressed.

The experience of guilt has always been one of the most excruciating problems in the history of mankind. It provides the plot for the great Greek dramas as well as for some of the best of modern film. All the great world religions have a substantial message about guilt and reconciliation; otherwise they would not have achieved their status. Christianity, too, addresses itself to this question. However, it is unique in its approach. In all other religions, it is man who reconciles the godhead to himself by penance, atonement, sacrifice (even as far as sacrifice of children). In Christianity it is *God* who reconciles. Justification is a free gift of God's grace (Rom 3:24) offered to us with the urgent appeal to be kind enough to accept this gift of reconciliation from the silver plate on which it is offered. It is God's initiative, God's longing.

This reconciliation does not mean that God was finally appeased when his Son died on the cross. The Son was not sent to satisfy the *Father* but rather to convince *us:*

> The unfortunate representation of the divine economy in terms of God's justice. . .has left not a few Christians with a caricature of God the Father, as a sort of celestial Shylock demanding his pound of flesh from man in the person of his own Son. The Gospel writers know nothing of this; in fact the entire New Testament knows nothing of this.[3]

The whole Old Testament is one long story of God's willingness to forgive, of his eagerness to restore his chosen people to their dignity and happiness, of his "emeth" as the reliability and faithfulness of his love. Paul's letter to Timothy gives us, indeed, an excellent summary of the message of all the prophets: "We may be unfaithful, but He is always faithful, for He cannot disown His own self" (2 Tim 2:13). But with all their unusual eloquence and their mighty personalities, the prophets did not succeed in conveying the message of complete acceptance notwithstanding the real guilt of the people. But God's love persisted: "At various times in the past and in various different ways God spoke to our ancestors through the prophets, but in our own time, the last days, He has spoken to us through His son" (Heb 1:1-2). Or, as Christ himself puts it in the parable of the wicked husbandmen: "He had still someone left: his beloved son. He sent him to them last of all. 'They will respect my son,' he said" (Mk 12:6). The mission of the Son was to show that God's love is greater than all our guilt, that though we have sinned, we are accepted: "I was born for this. I came into the world for this: to bear witness to the truth" (Jn 18:37). We recall once more that "truth" in the biblical sense means: the reliability of God's love. He fulfilled his mission by accepting everybody whom he met. The tax collector, the prostitute, the adulteress, the publican—all found in him the gentle sympathy that made each feel accepted. He did not break the crushed reed nor did he quench the wavering flame. He found something good in everyone and he condemned no one: "God sent His Son into the world, not to condemn the world but so that through Him the world might be saved" (Jn 3:17). He went out of his way to accept people who were oppressed by guilt. No one was let down by Christ. No one was too wicked in his eyes. He really was love enfleshed in a hardened world. His call exacted a great amount of loneliness because, when a man accepts everybody, then he belongs to nobody. Since Christ never rejected anybody, he did not belong to any of the groups and factions of his society: "Mine is not a kingdom of this world; if my kingdom were of this world, my men would have fought to prevent my being surrendered to the Jews. But my kingdom is not of this kind" (Jn 18:36). When he realized that his "open ethics" made him lonely, he still remained faithful to his mission. Even when it became evident that eventually everybody would turn against him, and that even his life was in danger, he nevertheless continued his universal acceptance. And when he died on the cross, mocked and hurt by gloating masochists, he accepted his torturers in the magnificent and heroic prayer: "Father, forgive them, they do not know what they are doing" (Lk 23:34). It was not the Father who demanded the cruel death of his Son. It was mankind that went that far in testing the genuineness of Christ's "open ethics" and universal acceptance. Man pushed it to that extreme. God did not charge man for the reconciliation but man charged God for it.

The centurion, the Roman officer who had been assigned to the crucifixion and who had watched it from beginning to end, was so impressed by the way in which Christ died that he grasped the super-human nature of this man. In his entire army career he had never come across anything like it: "The centurion who was standing in front of him, had seen how he had died and he said, 'In truth, this man was a son of God' " (Mk 15:39).[4] His eyes were opened in that ultimate test in which Christ was tried by his fellow-men.

When God's love revealed in Christ goes to that extreme, then it may dawn on us, too, that there really is no limit to God's love. It indeed transcends all our human thoughts. It is greater than our hearts and greater than our guilt. It may convince us that not "any created thing can come between us and the love of God made visible in Christ Jesus our Lord" (Rom 8:39). It may finally bring home to us that even with our real guilt we can still approach God and be sure of his acceptance. That is to experience a new birth, a new creation. When a man feels condemned, his creativity and his power to love, his joy in life as well as his sense of wholeness are blocked. When that same man suddenly or gradually understands that he is not rejected or condemned but accepted and loved by another on whom he depends, he experiences the refreshment of a healing stream. Everything is changed. There is sunshine again, and song. He can be glad and spread his happiness. Now he can give and love. He is a new man, a new creation. Things which were impossible when he felt condemned are now possible. It was the mission of Christ to bring man to that reconciliation and rebirth. Those who grasp that message, or rather, those to whom this event happens, we call Christians.

Eight

THE CELEBRATION OF HEALING

"Jesus also said, 'A man had two sons. The younger said to his father, "Father, let me have the share of the estate that would come to me." So the father divided the property between them. A few days later, the younger son got together everything that he had and left for a distant country where he squandered his money on a life of debauchery. When he had spent it all, that country experienced a severe famine, and now he began to feel the pinch, so he hired himself out to one of the local inhabitants who put him on his farm to feed the pigs' " (Lk 15:11-16). Contrary to Jewish custom, the father divided the property between his two sons. Perhaps the father consented to his son's choice to prevent a greater rebellion which would make his return all the more difficult or to evidence a disinterested respect for the free will of his son.

The consequences which the son suffered show clearly the consequences of sin. His experiences were empty. He squandered everything, even his future. Misery piled upon misery—he had no money, no food, no friends, no rest, no peace. He was shattered. As long as he had money, he had "friends;" when the money was gone, the "friends" disappeared, too. There is never any deep satisfaction or fruitfulness in the experience of sin. We know this. Yet so often we try it again. The effects of sin stretch far beyond the individual who commits the evil. The boy's stupidity brought sorrow to his home and caused the loss of the good name of his family. And, sadder than all this, it broke the heart of a loving father.

"Then he came to his senses and said, 'How many of my father's paid servants have more food than they want, and here am I dying of hunger! I will leave this place and go to my father and say: Father, I have sinned against heaven and against you; I no longer deserve to be called your son; treat me as one of your paid servants'. So he left the place and went back to his father " (v 17-20). It was physical hunger which brought the boy to his senses and made him return home. It was not a lofty motive, but it was an effective one. His hunger was a grace. It brought him to a real confession. Man's heart craves to be made whole, to be healed, to be cleansed and made new. This craving can be a strong urge to make a fresh start.

Without any excuses, the boy confessed: "Father, I have sinned. . ." The Gospel pushes aside all rationalizations. Sometimes our confessions are so empty. We so often stop where we should start! Rather than go to the depth, we remain on the surface. Our rebellion against God is always disguised. We have too much education, too much religious training to rebel openly. To be fruitful, our confessions must break through that facade.

The boy expressed real repentance. It was both vertical—"against heaven"—and horizontal—"against you". And he came home to express it. This is the difference between remorse and repentance. Remorse is a monologue. We feel sorry, but we do not express our sorrow. And because we never express it, we become despondent, downhearted. The classic example of this is Judas who betrayed his Lord but refused to confess his sin. He did not think that forgiveness was possible. Repentance is a dialogue. The sin is expressed. Peter, like Judas, also betrayed his Lord, but Peter confessed his sin, and he was forgiven.

Part of true repentance is that we learn our place: "I no longer deserve to be called your son; treat me as one of your paid servants." The boy made no claims. Everything now was a gift, and he was grateful. In a resolute way and against all human respect, he went home to tell his father he had sinned:

> The sacrament, the life of penance which is but the life of Christ lived out continually, is the most personal of all the sacraments, the most intense and, therefore, the most difficult. Perhaps it is the last sacrament we are ready for because it demands so much of us; it demands such maturity, it demands such a capacity to suffer, the most terrible kind of suffering, to really learn who we are. We will do anything to escape that kind of suffering, that kind of anguish. Who of us is really ready to face the living God?[1]

"While he was still a long way off, his father saw him and was moved with pity. He ran to the boy, clasped him in his arms and kissed him tenderly. Then his son said, 'Father, I have sinned against heaven and against you. I no longer deserve to be called your son.' But the father said to his servants, 'Quick! Bring out the best robe and put it on him; put a ring on his finger and sandals on his feet. Bring the calf we have been fattening, and kill it; we are going to have a feast, a celebration, because this son of mine was dead and has come back to life; he was lost and is found.' And they began to celebrate" (v 20-24). As he wound his way home, no doubt the boy wondered, "What will my father say?", "How will he react?". And, indeed, the father's reaction surpassed all expectations. Moved with pity, the father restored everything to his son—the robe, the ring, the sandals. He healed the wound. We sometimes meet people who have been hurt but have not yet been healed. These people often become bitter. They ruin their personalities. This is why the personal and explicit confession of sins is so important. The problem is not on God's side, but on ours. God forgives very easily and readily, but it is difficult for us to absorb his forgiveness. God responds quickly, infinitely fast, but we are slow, especially to recuperate from wounds of guilt. It is a gradual, all-encompassing process to be imbued with re-acceptance after the realization of real guilt. It is not rare to meet people who have confessed their sins, and who know intellectually that their sins are forgiven, but the wound has not yet healed. Herein lies the psychological root of the sacrament of penance. If we do not verbalize our sin in a conversation with a fellowman and hear his absolution spoken in the name of God, the forgiveness may not reach the heart. We have to express our guilt, and we cannot do that alone. This implies an important task for the confessor as well. He should give the penitent the opportunity to talk out his guilt without belittling it and without rushing him. (This is not a plea for any undue curiosity on his part.) Secondly, he should instill in the heart of the penitent God's forgiveness in such a way that it not only forgives but also heals.

God forgives in the blinking of an eye, but human beings need more time and help to be liberated from their guilt.

Perhaps we are so used to hearing this parable that we fail to sense how exceptional was the father's reaction. What human father would be able to react in such a way? What human father could be free of all resentment against the real guilt of his son and the hurt it caused to himself, that he could love him so completely without complaint? This is so foreign to the human experience that we have great trouble believing that this is the way God behaves towards us. How many of us are not caught in the dilemma: either our guilt is real and then God cannot possibly love us, or God really loves us but then our guilt is not real. The parable of the prodigal son breaks through that dilemma. It tries to convince us that "my thoughts are not your thoughts" (Is 55:6). It helps us in a powerful way to overcome our petty way of thinking about God's reaction to our guilt. The father set down no conditions nor did he demand a heart-to-heart talk. There were no strings attached. That is the way in which he won his son back completely. And this was the happiest day in the father's life—the day of the son's return. All of Luke 15—the parables of the lost sheep, the lost drachma, the lost son—tells of the joy of the father. It is this joy which is the basic reason for confession. We make God happy when we give him a chance to forgive us! Our confessions give God an opportunity to be God, to practice his faithfulness: "Let's have a celebration."

"Now the elder son was out in the fields and on his way back, as he drew near the house, he could

75

hear music and dancing. Calling one of the servants he asked what it was all about. 'Your brother has come' replied the servant, 'and your father has killed the calf we had fattened because he has got him back safe and sound.' He was angry then and refused to go in, and his father came out to plead with him; but he answered his father, 'Look, all these years I have slaved for you and never once disobeyed your orders, yet you never offered me so much as a kid for me to celebrate with my friends. But, for this son of yours, when he comes back after swallowing up your prop-erty—he and his women—you kill the calf we had been fattening.' The father said, 'My son, you are with me always and all I have is yours. But it was only right we should celebrate and rejoice, because your brother here was dead and has come to life; he was lost and is found' " (v 25-32). Up until now the younger son had been the black sheep of the family, the one who had gone astray whereas the elder son had remained close to his father. In the process of forgiveness, this order is changed com-pletely. The last one becomes the first. In being forgiven, the younger son learned to know his father in a very intimate way. The experience of God's forgiveness does indeed create a special bond between God and the one forgiven. This is an aspect of the Good News: that sin will not be held against us but, on the contrary, can be turned into an advantage. So great is the strength of God's healing power that the evil is turned into good.

In his refusal to join in the celebration, the son appealed to his years of service to the father. This is a dangerous appeal because there can be quite a bit of self in our service. Yet this is not the point of the parable. Jesus concentrates on the goodness of the father—the response of the father, the love of the father, the willingness of the father to forgive. It is not centered on the love of the sons and, really, there isn't too much love there. The first one came home because he was hungry and the other complained because he had never been given a kid to celebrate with his friends. To focus too much on our service and our achievements can make us complacent in a shallow or despondent way. It is better that we should focus on God, his love: "This is the love I mean: not our love for God, but God's love for us" (1 Jn 4:10). Let us look at the love of God and be happy. Let's celebrate!

Nine

GIVE THEM AN IMPRESSION OF WHO I AM

A king wished to see the son of a couple who lived near the bend in the river, ten miles upstream from the palace. He notified his ministers of his desire, and shortly thereafter they sent a messenger in the direction indicated. He reached a little farm where he found a young woman feeding the pigs. When the messenger conveyed the request of the king, the woman looked at him in astonishment. "There must be some mistake," she said. "I have no children at all, let alone a son who could speak with the king." So the servant returned to the palace empty-handed and reported his failure. The royal household, fearing the king's anger, hoped that the king would forget about his demand. Indeed, that seemed to be the case, since neither that day nor on those following did he again refer to the order.

One morning, about twenty-five years later, a young man appeared at the gate of the palace. It was obvious that he was wearing his best clothes since his rustic appearance and simple demeanor were out of harmony with the solemn dark blue apparel he was wearing. He asked to see the king who had supposedly summoned him. The gate-keeper eyed him with suspicion and, a little later, the footman declared that the king had not summoned the boy.

The boy insisted, and finally was permitted a hearing by the highest officials of the court. An elderly councillor recognized the story of the boy who told how, long before his birth, a messenger from the palace had come with the request of the king to see him. When the chief master of ceremonies, with a great show of words, asked the king if he would like to receive the young man, the king, with surprise on his face, said that he, himself, had asked the boy to come, hadn't he?

So the young farmer's son met his master. The conversation which followed was even stranger than the story told thus far. The king stood up, clasped the young man's hand, ordered everyone else to leave the hall, and seated the boy before his throne. Then he said, "My kingdom is large. It extends far beyond the home of your parents, and one may walk for hours before he can reach its boundaries. My people live in many scattered areas; few of them have seen me, and they have only a vague idea of what a king is like. I entrust to you a mission: to give my people an impression of who I am. Here! I give you a sceptre, a crown, and a royal robe. Go in peace."

The king stood up, leaving the boy awed and confused, sitting in the chair. In his hands he held a tiny crown, a sceptre, and a royal robe hardly large enough for a little doll.

Before the king left the hall, the boy recovered his senses enough to say in a hushed voice, "But I do not know you at all." The king paid no attention. In a louder, braver tone, the boy called out, "But what exactly am I supposed to do?" The king had departed. In wild despair, the boy shouted, "Why do I have to do this?" A footman entered, bowed to him, and ushered him out of the throne room. A moment later the boy found himself outside in the midday sun. Slowly he returned to his home, pondering over the strange things that had happened.

On his return home, he recounted the whole story to his parents who were delighted that their son had been received by the king and had spoken with him. They spread the story abroad to all their relatives, friends, and neighbors. The son, however, constantly thought about his mission. Whether he was working in the fields or resting from his labors, he was haunted by thoughts of the king's orders.

Finally, he decided to visit the wise man of the village. Having heard the story and the problems which worried the young man, the wise man gave him this advice: "Of course, you know what a king is, but you don't know about this particular king because you have met him only once. Perhaps the circumstances of your summons to the court and the manner in which the king received you may hold some clues. Moreover, I shouldn't be surprised if the scepter, the crown, and the royal robe might be symbolic of the character of the king himself. Perhaps if you take time to consider the royal gifts attentively, you may discover their meaning. Once you have solved this mystery, try to be as the hidden message of robe, and scepter, and crown indicate you should be."

The boy nodded. It seemed a good plan. "Still," he protested, "How am I to earn a living?" "You are a farmer," said the wise man. "Remain one. There is nothing worse than a farmer playing the role of an executive, or a clerk playing the role of a landlord.

81

Had this been the right way, the king himself would have come to work in your fields."

With a sigh, the young farmer said, "But why did the king ask *me* to fulfill this mission?" The wise man smiled, and replied, "Simply because the king could just as well have asked somebody else."

Thus it came about that, close to the river, there lived a man whom all the people loved. He was wise and just, and it was a pleasure to deal with him. This man sowed and reaped his wheat, fed his pigs, and fertilized his lands. From time to time, someone would come to visit him. Why? Nobody could explain exactly why. It was as if, in his presence, one became more himself. It was as if one who had been hungry became satisfied. Among themselves, the people discussed mysterious sayings which they had heard from him. Once, while on an evening walk in the fields with some friends, he had said, "The grain of wheat dies, and life comes up. We need not fear death." There was another of his sayings which struck people every time. It was: "In the midst of all that disappears, one thing remains—namely that one has been loved."

Then, one day, he died. After his passing, his nephews and nieces began to look for his treasures. They had heard, in the family tradition, that he had once received from the king a scepter, crown and robe of pure gold. In all their searching, they found only a worn book which began with these strange words: "The geneology of Jesus Christ, the son of Abraham, the son of David. . .".[1]

Explanation of the Parable

The Call: Our parable has a strange beginning: a boy is told to visit the king before he is even born! But, strange as this may seem, we find the exact experience written on the pages of Scripture: "Before I formed you in the womb I knew you; before you came to birth I consecrated you" (Jer 1:5), and "Yahweh called me before I was born, from my mother's womb he pronounced my name" (Is 49:1) and again, "Then God who had specially chosen me while I was still in my mother's womb called me through his grace and chose to reveal His Son in me, so that I might preach the Good News about him to the pagans" (Gal 1:15-16). The mission entrusted to the prophets and to St. Paul is the mission given to each of us. Long before we were born, God sent a messenger. He had a call for us.

After the message has been sent, the king waits twenty-five years for the boy to come. Twenty-five years of waiting is nothing for God. He is patient. He has a profound respect for each of us. He also expects that one day we will come. That is why the king is surprised when the master of ceremonies with much flurry asks if he still desires to see the boy:

"Of course I do! I asked him to come, didn't I?"

This is God's way. He gives us unbounded trust and confidence. He has no doubts. And when one has no doubts, one can be patient.

The Mission: The boy's mission is to give the people an impression of who the king is. This is the

83

vocation given to each one of us—to give the people an impression of who Christ is: "If you come back, I will take you back into my service; and if you utter noble, not despicable, thoughts, you shall be as my mouth" (Jer 15:19). We are to speak what we have learned from the Lord: "The Lord Yahweh has given me a disciple's tongue" (Is 50:4). We do not have to bring our own message, our own thoughts. We do not have to impose ourselves. We have only to speak the word of the Lord, to become transparent for the Lord. To convey the Gospel is a creative work. We have first to give it shape in our own lives. Only in this way do we communicate the message of God. We teach who Christ is by living Christ: "They are the ones he chose specially long ago and intended to become true images of His Son. . ." (Rom 8:29). True images of the Son—this is our vocation. We should be a reference to Christ, a word referring to "The Word."

The Questions (asked by those who are called): "But I do not know you at all." The knowledge of Christ is fundamental to our mission. How can we give people an impression of who Christ is if we ourselves do not know him? For this knowledge we must sacrifice everything:

> I believe nothing can happen that will outweigh the supreme advantage of knowing Christ Jesus my Lord. For Him I have accepted the loss of everything, and I look on everything as so much rubbish if only I can have Christ and be given a place in Him (Phil 3:7-8).

To know Christ must be the goal of our lives. And the only way to know Christ is to contemplate him: "And we with our unveiled faces reflecting like mirrors the brightness of the Lord, all grow brighter and brighter as we are turned into the image that we reflect; this is the work of the Lord who is Spirit" (2 Cor 3:18). Gradually, imperceptibly, something happens and we are transformed into the image that we contemplate. This is indeed "the work of the Lord who is Spirit." The process is a long one. It takes time—time wasted in prayer. There is no other way to know Christ.

"But what exactly am I supposed to do?" In one sense there is no answer to this question except simply to concentrate on Christ: "It was by faith that Abraham obeyed the call to set out for a country that was the inheritance given to him and his descendants, and that he set out without knowing where he was going" (Heb 11:8). We, too, must set out without knowing where we are going. We need only follow Christ and cling to him. We do not know where he will lead us. We do not have to know that. We shouldn't even need to know that. This is basic to faith. When we have our lives all figured out, there is no need to believe! No, we follow Christ. He is the way we go, the path we walk.

The wise man, however, does give some practical advice: "Perhaps the circumstances of your summons to the court and the manner in which the king received you may hold some clues." The way in which the Lord calls us may indeed give a clue. The history of every person's vocation is unique. It is beautiful, even wonderful, how God calls each of us and enables us to accept and live it. It is good to ponder on this. The best way of renewal is to return to beginnings, to touch once again the original inspiration. Again, the wise man suggested that the boy study the gifts he had received from the king: the crown which is a crown of thorns, the scepter which is in the form of a cross, the robe which is the robe that Christ wore when he was mocked by Herod's soldiers. These three symbols imply a life of suffering and of ridicule. Only through suffering can we express who Christ is. To image Christ we must be willing to follow the way of the cross.

"But why did the king ask *me* to fulfill this mission?" And the wise man answered, "Simply because the king could just as well have asked somebody else." God does not love us for what we are, but we are because he loves us. His call is creative. Since he calls us, he enables us to be fruitful: "You did not choose me; no, I chose you and I commissioned you to go out and to bear fruit, fruit that will last" (Jn 15:16). In his choice, he gives each of us the possibility of bearing fruit—his fruit—that will last.

"How am I to earn a living?" And the reply is: "You are a farmer; remain one." We shouldn't try to be important in our call. We shouldn't think that since we have a vocation, we should be able to do anything. We should humbly accept our limitations and not go beyond them. Much harm is done when we do not accept our limitations of health, of intelligence and of other talents as well.

Conclusions: "It was as if, in his presence, one became more himself." This is the sign of a holy man. He gives people the good feeling of being themselves. There is no pressure, no uneasiness. Pressure always implies a lack of respect, a lack of love. This is not God's way. If we are to express Christ to the people, we must give them the feeling that they are always welcome to be themselves.

"In the midst of all that disappears, one thing remains—namely, that one has been loved." It is more important to have been loved than to love. It is deeper, more original. First, we must be loved before we can love. This is the basic reality: "This is the love I mean: not our love for God, but God's love for us" (1 Jn 4:10). And it is the one reality that remains: God's truth, God's reliability.

The young man's nieces and nephews searched for the secret of his vocation. But they failed to find it. The secret of a vocation is personal. It cannot be handed down from generation to generation. It can only be passed on through the Gospel. And then, it will begin all over again.

Ten

OUR YES AND AMEN

Introduction: The baptism of Jesus marks the beginning of his public life. The Gospels too begin with the proclamation of the baptism of Christ.[1] The event of the baptism contains the whole Gospel in a nutshell. It is like the overture of an opera. It is the frontispiece of an unusual book: the presentation of Jesus to Christian believers. For Christ, the baptism was the key moment of his life. He had lived thirty years in preparation for it; he would need the rest of his life to fulfill it. He knew it encompassed all that was foretold by the prophets concerning the servant of Yahweh. For the Father as well as for the Son, it was an intense moment. As in a kind of sacrament, Christ received and accepted his mission from the Father. He submitted himself to the task his Father gave him. Officially, he said "Yes" to the Father with the full realization of what that "Yes" implied. He placed his entire life—what was and is to come—into the hands of the Father.

Beginning: "Then Jesus appeared: he came from Galilee to the Jordan to be baptised by John" (Mt 3:13). According to tradition, Jesus is thirty years old when he comes to the Jordan. He has lived those thirty years in Nazareth. His mother has wondered at times "Is this the child announced by the angel?"

89

There are no signs of a kingdom, no throne of his ancestor David. Then one day Jesus tells his mother that he must leave. It breaks his heart to tell her, but he has to leave home. His Father wants him elsewhere. And Mary knows that the Father means everything to her Son. She had learned it the hard way when the boy of only twelve years replied to her in the Temple of Jerusalem: "Did you not know I must be busy with my Father's affairs?" (Lk 2:49). She did not understand then, but gradually she realizes how much the will of the Father is the backbone, the nerve of her Son's life. And Mary does not wish to interfere. She herself had said "Let it be done according to your will." She wants the Word of God to happen in her life. Even if it means that Jesus leaves home, she wants the Father's will to be accomplished. Jesus thanks his mother and she in turn thanks him for all that he has been to her—the content of her life. He is a lonely man now. He belongs to nobody, to no family, to no village:

> The spirit of the Lord has been given to me, for he has anointed me.
> He has sent me to bring the good news to the poor, to proclaim liberty to captives and to the blind new sight, to set the downtrodden free, to proclaim the Lord's year of favor (Lk 4:18).

He belongs to all—to the poor, the blind, the captives, the outcasts—and that means he is lonely. It is the loneliness of belonging to everybody. Gandhi once said, "If you want to be a friend of God, you must either stay alone or be a friend of the whole world." And it seems that these two are the same. This is the loneliness which Christ now experiences.

90

He appears at the Jordan where John the Baptist is preaching and baptizing, and joins the crowd. He listens to John. Here is a kindred soul. In him, Jesus recognizes his own spirituality and decides to be baptized by John.

The Baptism: The baptism of John is a baptism of repentance and of forgiveness of sin. He does not baptize people who wish to join the Jewish religion. He baptizes those who are already Jews but Jews in need of conversion. It is a second call. And John is severe in his preaching. To be a son of Abraham means nothing. One has to change one's life, to admit one's sinfulness. This is what John preaches. Jesus lines up with the crowd and waits his turn. He lays no claim to anything special. He asks no exceptions. In effect, Jesus joins us. He chooses to share our life, to live in solidarity with mankind. Solidarity, for Christ, is not just to mix with the crowd, to socialize, but to share our guilt and sinfulness. John is shocked: "John tried to dissuade him. 'It is I who need baptism from you,' he said, 'and yet you come to me!' But Jesus replied, 'Leave it like this for the time being; it is fitting that we should, in this way, do all that righteousness demands.' At this, John gave in to him" (Mt 3:14-15). Christ insists. He wants to be baptized. He wants to be treated like a sinner. This public act of solidarity will extend beyond the limits of the moment, beyond the shores of the Jordan. Eventually this solidarity will turn Christ completely into sin: "For our sake God made the sinless one into sin so that in him we might become the goodness of God" (2 Cor 5:21). When Christ is baptized he is fully

91

aware that his baptism means his life, his death. This is the most costly act he can perform. Later, when he refers to his baptism, he will always mean his death: "There is a baptism I must still receive, and how great is my distress till it is over" (Lk 12:50). His whole life is at stake.

"As soon as Jesus was baptised, he came up from the water, and suddenly the heavens opened and he saw the Spirit of God descending like a dove and coming down on him. And a voice spoke from heaven, 'This is my Son, the Beloved; my favor rests on him' " (Mt 3:16-17). Matthew ends the account of the baptism with a phrase from the Old Testament. It is the first verse from the first song of the servant of Yahweh: "Here is my servant whom I uphold, my chosen one in whom my soul delights" (Is 42:1). For John, too, the baptism and songs of the servant of Yahweh are bound together. John condenses his account of the baptism into these words: "I saw the Spirit coming down on him from heaven like a dove and resting on him" (Jn 1:32) and we read in the first song of the servant of Yahweh: "I have endowed him with my spirit" (Is 42:1). The Jews knew the Scriptures. One line was sufficient to quote a whole chapter. They were familiar with the prophecies telling of the coming Messiah. The four songs of the servant of Yahweh give a clear description of "the one who is to come" (Mt 11:3). Christ knew them by heart. He had meditated on them, pondered well the realities they foretold: 1). The servant is sent by Yahweh to fulfill a mission. The initiative is Yahweh's. The servant listens and then obeys: "Each morning he wakes me to hear, to listen like a disciple. The Lord Yahweh has opened my ear" (Is 50:4). 2). The servant is sent to serve the people, to liberate them: "He does not break the crushed reed, nor quench the wavering flame" (Is 42:3). He will be gentle. He will help the people. To be sent and to serve are closely interrelated. Because the Son is so completely surrendered to the Father, he is available to all mankind. Because he is so open to the Father, the love of the Father can flow through him and enable him to be the man for others. 3). The servant will pay the price—the complete giving of oneself. The fourth song (Is 52:13-53:12) tells of the hard life of the servant of Yahweh, the tremendous sufferings he will undergo.

> Without beauty, without majesty (we saw him),
> no looks to attract our eyes;
> a thing despised and rejected by men,
> a man of sorrows and familiar with suffering,
> a man to make people screen their faces;
> he was despised and we took no account of him (Is 53:3).

4). The servant's life, because of the suffering, will be fruitful. His fruitfulness will fill the whole world; all nations will benefit from it. Newman once remarked, "Good is never done except at the expense of those who do it." When Jesus is baptized, he accepts the four songs. He knows what is to be fulfilled and he tells his Father "Yes, if this is my mission, I accept it." Jesus empties himself.

Matthew points out that Jesus did not follow the ordinary ritual of baptism. The Jews would come to the edge of the river, bow their heads, and then immerse themselves in the water. After the immersion, they would stand still and confess their sins. Then they would leave. As soon as Jesus was baptized, he emerged from the waters and left. There was no confession of personal sins. Instead, there was a confession from heaven: "And a voice spoke from heaven, 'This is my Son, the Beloved; my favor rests on him' " (Mt 3:17). Christ emptied himself. Now he is glorified by the Father:

His state was divine, yet he did not cling to his equality with God

but emptied himself to assume the condition of a slave, and became as men are;

and being as all men are, he was humbler yet, even to accepting death, death on a cross.

But God raised him high and gave him the name which is above all other names

so that all beings in the heavens, on earth and in the underworld, should bend the knee at the name of Jesus and that every tongue should acclaim Jesus Christ as Lord, to the glory of God the Father (Phil 2:6-11).

The life of Christ which is summarized in this hymn of the early Church was foretold in prophecy at the baptism event. There Christ emptied himself, joining in solidarity with our sinfulness; therefore, he was glorified by the Father. The Father is pleased with his Son. At last, after so many disappointed hopes, he has found a man who is capable of accomplishing the work that was planned since the creation of the world. He will tell the people of the Father, of his love and acceptance of them. He will pay the price on demand, but he will succeed.

"Then Jesus was led by the Spirit out into the wilderness to be tempted by the devil" (Mt 4:1). This fullness of the Spirit is part of the baptism of Jesus: "God had anointed him with the Holy Spirit and with power, and because God was with him, Jesus went about doing good and curing all who had fallen into the power of the devil" (Acts: 10:38). The Spirit of God which is so powerful in the Old Testament (see Genesis 1) means life—"Ruach Yahweh." The Spirit of God which strengthened the leaders of Israel (the prophets and kings), and the power which led them are concentrated in Christ. He is full of God; he radiates God. So much fullness of the Father and the Spirit does he possess that in him we encounter and experience God himself.

Our Baptism: Our baptism shares the same elements of emptying and glorification, of death and life:

> You have been taught that when we were baptized in Christ Jesus we were baptized in his death; in other words, when we were baptized we went into the tomb with him and joined in death, so that as Christ was raised from the dead by the Father's glory, we too might live a new life (Rom 6:3-4).

We share the death of Christ. We empty ourselves. We enter the tomb. And in this way, we join Christ in his resurrection. We know the power of his resurrection and the peace that it brings with it. We experience the fruitfulness of a new life which is no longer bound to the past. New strength envelops us. Our baptism means that we open ourselves to Christ so that his life may continue through us.

Eleven

NEITHER DO I CONDEMN YOU

". . .as all the people came to Jesus, he sat down and began to teach them" (Jn 8:2). We gather with these people to listen to the Word of God:

> The word of the Lord is perfect,
> source of life.
> What he promises is pure truth,
> only peace.
> And as exquisite as honey,
> no, still more—
> far more precious than pure gold
> is the Lord's own word (Ps 19:7,9,10).[1]

Like Mary who was completely open and receptive to the word of God we want to open ourselves:

> I want to hear the word of the Lord.
> Peace—that is the word of the Lord (Ps 85:8).[2]

Like Mary we want to let all of God's word through so that our lives, too, become a blessing, a grace to this world. In the Word, God has said everything he has to say. When God seems silent, it is because he has already spoken and there is nothing else to add. He only wants us to listen more intently to that word which we never fully grasp. We have in our "instant" society an enormous expenditure of

97

words. We combine letters and sounds—new words—which within a decade are obsolete! But the Word of God is hard-wearing, indeed it is everlasting. We can only listen to that word when we are willing to offer our whole being to God: "None of you can be my disciple unless he gives up all his possessions" (Lk 14:33).

"The scribes and Pharisees brought a woman along who had been caught committing adultery; and making her stand there in full view of everybody, they said to Jesus, 'Master, this woman was caught in the very act of committing adultery.' " (Jn 8:3-4). The Pharisees hold in full view not a woman any more but a thing, a case. They are not interested in the person. They make no attempt to understand, to show concern. They simply condemn. " 'And Moses has ordered us in the Law to condemn women like this to death by stoning. What have you to say?' They asked him this as a test, looking for something to hold against him" (v 5-6a). The Pharisees use the law to trap this woman, to kill her. Even worse, they use a human being to trap Jesus and to kill him. This woman is just an instrument in their schemes to condemn Jesus. They are not interested in justice, and Jesus knows this. He remains silent. "But Jesus bent down and started writing on the ground with his finger. As they persisted with their question, he looked up and said, 'If there is one of you who has not sinned, let him be the first to throw a stone at her.' Then he bent down and wrote on the ground again" (v 6b-8). Jesus used his finger not to accuse but to write on the ground. That is innocuous. What is written on the ground can be quickly scuffed away.

He makes it clear that all of us are sinners. The more or less that means so much to us does not concern him. We have to know that we live on his forgiveness. "When they heard this they went away one by one, beginning with the eldest, until Jesus was left alone with the woman, who remained standing there. He looked up and said, 'Woman, where are they? Has no one condemned you?' 'No one, Sir,' she replied. 'Neither do I condemn you'" (v 9-11). This must have been a tremendous moment in her life. She was really close to death. In fact, according to the law she was already condemned to death by stoning. Jesus rescued her from the gates of death. No one was interested in this woman. But Jesus was. Finally, there comes into her life one person who accepts her, who approaches her as a human being. Finally, there is someone who believes in her, and not in a condescending way. Christ is unreservedly receptive. This is a beautiful example of listening. Christ himself listens to this person. She says very little—'No one, Sir'—but Jesus listens even before she speaks. He who cannot understand a friend's silence, will never understand his words. To listen is much more difficult than to speak or to look. When I speak or look, I am the center, and this is natural to me. But when I listen, the other person becomes the center and that is much more demanding. To listen is to grab hold of my center of gravity and place it for a time in the other person. It requires great effort to do this for any length of time. It means to empty oneself in order to be filled with the other person. Christ emptied himself. He was and still is a master at listening, since in him there is no self-concern. He

99

listened to this woman and he understood all. " 'Go away, and don't sin any more' " (v 11). Christ told the woman that she had sinned. He said it without hurting her because he accepted her. Indeed it is a miracle that he could say "don't sin any more." He enabled her to overcome her sin not because he frightened or threatened her but because he accepted her. In the encounter with Christ, she was born anew, she could begin a new life:

No need to recall the past,
no need to think about what was done before.
See, I am doing a new deed,
even now it comes to light; can you not see it?
Yes, I am making a road in the wilderness,
paths in the wilds (Is 43:18-19).

Christ gives us a new future: "I have opened in front of you a door that nobody will be able to close" (Rev 3:8a) and the door is Christ himself. The experience of God's acceptance in Christ makes a new beginning possible.

Faith is "the courage to accept acceptance." That faith will bring about a metanoia, a conversion. The certainty we have is not in a thing but in a person—Jesus Christ. We can view evangelical perfection as a lofty ideal, infinitely far away and beyond our reach; in fact, as impossible. We can also envision the Gospel as a blueprint, something which we have to work out and to which we give all of our energies. This is a frustrating and joyless adventure! The day will come when we realize that we have not made any headway, that all the distances we have traveled do not count. The ideal is always infinitely distant. We may be tempted at this moment to give up. This would be a basic mistake for we confuse the Gospel with an ideology, with an ideal. The Gospel is a Person. Perfection means to follow Jesus Christ, to accept the friendship of Christ. There is no tension, no sense of guilt or failure. We go with Christ. We do not lose courage because we are with him. He accepts us as we are, and we accept ourselves. This is wholesome and liberating. Now we can concentrate on the desires of Christ. We do not have to be bothered with a blueprint. We can live in the presence of God, the sacrament of the present moment. There we can find God day by day. The ideal, then, is not a state of perfection to be reached but fidelity to God's love, the Providence of God. We are centered on a Person, not on an ideal. This makes all the difference in the world. We are more accepting of the failures and imperfections of ourselves and others. Each person goes his own way with Christ. We no longer need the subtle masks to hide our faults and to pretend non-existing virtues. The only criterion is sincerity in my relationship with Christ. This will give us peace and creativity and encouragement. This principle applies to a community as well. It means that we, the community, do not have to bridge the gap between the ideal and the reality. When we go with Christ, we do not have to pretend anything. We simply concentrate on fidelity to Jesus.

This is the biblical sense of perfection. It never implies a state of perfection to be reached by way of moral achievement. All through Scripture we read of the presence of God's glory and power in a place or in a person. This is to speak of perfection. Mt. Sinai was holy, because there the glory of Yahweh had descended and Yahweh was present in a very special way. The name "Yahweh" was a holy name because it professed the presence of Yahweh. Moses was a holy man because Yahweh was present to him in an unusual degree. This is always what holiness means: to open oneself to the living presence of God, to give up everything for this relationship:

> Not only that but I believe nothing can happen that will outweigh the supreme advantage of knowing Christ Jesus my Lord. For him I have accepted the loss of everything, and I look on everything as so much rubbish if only I can have Christ and be given a place in him (Phil 3:8-9).

This is Paul's idea of perfection. He wants to be with Christ. He is not building up himself. He is not achieving anything. The Gospel of Jesus does not mean the Gospel message which Jesus preached, the theory which he brought into this world. The Gospel of Jesus Christ means the Good News *that he is. His Person* is the Gospel. It is the message embodied in the person. This is the salvation of this woman: " 'Go away and don't sin any more.' " She can go away because she has encountered Christ, and she will never forget him. The encounter lasted but an instant, but so much happened. That man accepted her as she was at the very moment she was really lost. She will always go with him.

Twelve

THE IMPOSSIBILITY OF THE GOSPEL

One day a rich young man for whom eternal life was a burning question approached Jesus. He felt that this unusual rabbi knew the secret. He was not afraid. He had no human respect. He knelt down in the street before Jesus and asked: " 'Good Master, what must I do to inherit eternal life?' Jesus said to him, 'Why do you call me good?' " (Mk 10:17-18a). There is no concern in Jesus for his own glory. He cannot be trapped by titles: "Not that I care for my own glory, there is someone who takes care of that and is the judge of it" (Jn 8:50). He referred the young man to the Father: " 'No one is good but God alone,' " but at the same time he gave him an answer to his question: " 'You know the commandments: You must not kill; You must not commit adultery; You must not steal; You must not bring false witness; You must not defraud: Honour your father and mother' " (v 18b-19). So eternal life, for Jesus, is the service of God shaped through one's service to his fellowman. To this examination of conscience the young man replied: " 'Master, I have kept all these from my earliest day' " (v 20). What the youth is searching for now becomes clear. He is not asking about the commandments. He knows them and has always kept them. He is asking about the ultimate, the decisive element, his unique call in life. "Jesus looked steadily at him and loved him" (v 21). The love of the Father is reflected in the eyes of the Son. I cannot say that I have kept all the commandments from my youth, yet that same infinite love goes out to me as to this youth. The refrain "God saw that it was good" (Gen 1) becomes visible in Christ as he gazes in full confidence and sympathy on this young man. "Then Jesus said, 'There is one thing you lack. Go and sell everything you own and give the money to the poor' " (v 21). From his love comes an invitation—not an additional commandment but a concretization. Because Christ loves him so much, he offers him poverty. That is a gift, a special favor. How happy are the poor in spirit!

Christ wants this young man to be happy, and he knows that in poverty there is happiness, peace, joy—the kingdom of heaven on earth! The value of poverty is a mystery. It can only be discerned from the inside by experience. Once it is compromised, one is no longer happy. Poverty makes the spiritual life easier in every way. When one is poor one relies on God for everything. Jesus touches this young man exactly where he is most vulnerable and this is the radicalism of the Gospel: "Then Jesus said to his disciples, 'If anyone wants to be a follower of mine, let him renounce himself and take up his cross and follow me. For anyone who wants to save his life will lose it; but anyone who loses his life for my sake will find it. What, then, will a man gain if he wins the whole world and ruins his life? Or what has a man to

104

offer in exchange for his life?' " (Matt 16:24-26). I can read this and similar passages of the Gosepl and still maintain a comfortable existence as long as I keep it at a distance and remain uninvolved. But in his invitation to poverty Christ specifies the radical call for this particular man. The Gospel is always meant to be specific. The invitation of Christ is always personal. Knowing he had touched a sore spot in this young man's heart, Jesus added " 'and you will have treasure in heaven.' " Christ reveals to the young man the secret to eternal life. Who would choose poverty if he doesn't see the mystery in it, the richness of it? The poor in spirit possess the kingdom of God right now. They are a life-time ahead of the others—the real avant-garde. They do, here and now, what everybody will have to do in the evening of life. They give up all their possessions because they have found God or in order to find him. " 'Then come, follow me' " (v 21). The following of Christ is a reward for poverty, or poverty is a condition for the following of Christ: "None of you can be my disciple unless he gives up all his possessions" (Lk 14:33). Every time I must try again. To this young man who brought his most crucial question about life to Christ, who even knelt before him in the street, Jesus offers his friendship. That is the strongest incentive Christ can offer him. If he is afraid of his own weakness, Christ will always go first. His example will be power enough to draw him. It isn't an empty poverty to which the young man is called but a poverty *because of* and *with* Christ. "But his face fell at these words and he went away sad, for he was a man of great wealth" (v 22). The young man's face flooded with disappointment. His whole demeanor shrank. His eyes lowered their gaze and his shoulders drooped. Slowly the disappointment filled his heart and took hold of it. And one wonders: "Is he a man disappointed for life?" "Will he ever be happy the rest of his life?" "Will he ever be able to make anyone else happy?" Such a sad ending for so beautiful a beginning! The young man was saddened when Christ became specific. As long as the Gospel remains general, impersonal, it is no problem. But then it isn't Gospel: "And if there were a devil it would not be one who decided against God, but one who, in eternity, came to no decision."[1] The devil doesn't deny God. He leaves everything open. He doesn't commit himself. Christ asks the young man to commit himself in a specific way, and he is unwilling to do it. For he is a man of great wealth. How dangerous possessions are! He was possessed by what he owned. How easy it is to be gripped as by a slow poison and to lose the spirit of poverty which is detachment and freedom and truth:

> Let us not deceive ourselves and let us not dilute the most precious things Jesus said. To my friends I must say: beware of the temptation of riches. It is much more serious than it may appear today to well-intentioned Christians, and it sows destruction primarily because we underestimate its danger. Riches are slow poison, which strikes almost imperceptibly, paralyzing the soul at the moment it seems healthiest. They are thorns which grow with the grain and suffocate it right at the moment when the corn is beginning to shoot up. What number of men and women, religious people, let themselves get caught up in their later lives by the spirit of middle-class tastes.[2]

Poverty is a fragile treasure. One must be on his guard to keep it whole and wholesome: "Each of us should continue to ask: How is poverty a beatitude in my life and what have been its effects upon it? How have I led others to discover and to embrace the secret and gift of poverty?"[3] The man struggled for a moment in his heart, but his possessions meant more than anything else to him—even life itself!And he was disappointed. The apostles were disappointed, too! It wasn't often that a man who was young and rich and educated approached Jesus about his vocation. Why didn't Jesus permit him to join the group first and then gradually learn poverty from them? Jesus does not trust that type of approach. "Jesus looked around and said to his disciples, 'How hard it is for those who have riches to enter the kingdom of God.'" The apostles were really annoyed. "But Jesus insisted, 'My children,' he said to them, 'how hard it is to enter the kingdom of God! It is easier for a camel to pass through the eye of a needle than for a rich man to enter the kingdom of God'" (v 23-25). Jesus took the refusal of the young man to give up his possessions very seriously. Nobody can serve two masters. The decisive factor is whether, in that encounter with Christ, I come to the radical choice: that I acknowledge him as Lord, that he no longer has to share his lordship with any one or any thing. Of the ten lepers, only one returned to thank Christ. For this one leper—one out of ten—encounter with Christ was sufficient reason to change the direction of his life. The

107

apostles were more astounded than ever. " 'In that case,' they said to one another, 'who can be saved?' " (v 26). The apostles found Jesus hard to understand, and this time even impossible. Until I experience the impossibility of the Gospel, I cannot begin to live it. It really is impossible. It is so radical, so demanding, that I can never manage on my own. I can begin to follow Christ only when I realize that the Gospel is beyond my reach. When the moment arrives that I realize that it is too much—"I can't do it"—I begin to rely not on my own strength but on Christ. This is the real beginning of the Christian life. Everything up to this point was just the prelude. "Jesus gazed at them. 'For men,' he said, 'it is impossible, but not for God: Because everything is possible for God' " (v 27). I can build on the strength of God. He is my peace. He will accomplish the work he has begun if only I surrender myself to him and allow him his way.

Thirteen

HOW HAPPY ARE THE POOR IN SPIRIT

"How happy are the poor in spirit; theirs is the kingdom of heaven." (Mt 5:3).

How far is our world from understanding that that man is happy who is poor in spirit! Most of us live in a society which is more concerned with creating a market than with the product to be marketed. In the past, production served consumption: because the people needed bread, the baker set up his shop. In an affluent society, it is just the opposite: consumption serves the production. There is no industry which profits from asking itself "How can we serve the people?" The big question of industry today is "How can we create needs which will in turn expand our industry?" The consumer is kept under an aggressive pressure not to appease and satisfy his real needs but to buy whatever industry wants to sell for its own expansion. Industry manages to make products which in a matter of months are obsolete and out-of-date. This part of a car is no longer made. This model cannot be replaced and so on, ad nauseam! The trap we are all enmeshed in is the trap of overemphasized misplaced values. We would experience more freedom and happiness, less tension, if we could attribute less value to material things and status symbols, and give more attention to non-material goods such as better communication within the family, a faith-filled attitude as husband or wife or religious. Although we all live under the

109

tyranny of an affluent society, the poor seem to be its worst victims. Television advertising and the pressure of industry are much more effective with the poor than with the rich. Rich people know from their own experiences that not every day is filled with wine and roses. They know, too, that they may have all the luxuries and yet suffer from the unhappy realities of life, i.e., a broken marriage, estrangement from their children. More than likely the poor man does not realize this. He dreams of more money for more pleasures in the hope that there will be more happiness. With the vow of poverty the religious life should demonstrate to the poor how little is necessary to be truly happy. This is the witness that the religious owe the poor in these times. But then they have to take their vow seriously and live a poor life. Statistics remind us of the complexity of the problem, but where do we spend our energies? While two-thirds of the world is literally disease-ridden and starving for food, we cope with problems of obesity and pollution. Do we associate unreservedly with this one-third of the world's population and thus make the Gospel lose its credibility for the other two-thirds? To be poor means to go against the current: "If the world hates you, remember that it hated me before you. If you belonged to the world, the world would love you as its own" (Jn 15:18). It takes a foolish and humble person to live a poor life in this crazy world of ours.

Our problem is not poverty but the lack of it—and that is what makes us unhappy and creates our tensions. Some religious have sacrificed, on the altar of renewal and adaptation, their poverty and their inner life, their real vocation and their identity: "The one who received the seed in thorns is the man who hears the word, but the worries of this world and the lure of riches choke the word and so he produces nothing" (Mt 13:22). They have been manipulated. They are no longer free. What is sorely needed is a sincere renewal in poverty:

> It is in the nature of poverty to imply a constant renovation: without this action and the continual effort of disengagement, the usage of earthly possessions could soon lead to a state of comfortable establishment, of being bogged down. Poverty is a perpetual pilgrimage towards the absolute. . .but a pilgrimage which never attains its goal here below. We have to learn to inflict death on the desire of possession and on the slavery it involves. And this is a situation contrary to the need of independence which we all experience. Nevertheless it is there that the heart of evangelical poverty is to be found. [1]

Although the material aspect of poverty is not primary to the spirit neither can it be disregarded. It would be unrealistic and even a lack of poverty to claim unwittingly that one can be poor in spirit and not poor in practice: "In our pursuit of this difficult enterprise (of realizing poverty nowadays) it is well to recall that some kind of deprivation, consonant with the apostolic work of the religious order, is a staunch ally."[2] It appears that because we cannot solve the ulterior problems we neglect to take the immediate steps which would be within our reach. Because we fail to see how we can go all the way, we take no step at all: "I do not ask to see the distant scene; one step enough for me" (Cardinal Newman).

A bird's eye glance at the evolution of the concept of poverty through the Old Testament may recycle our thought and set our sights on new horizons. In the beginning of the Old Testament wealth was considered a sign of God's special blessing. The possessions of Abraham and Moses, the heritage David left to Solomon were proofs of Yahweh's favor for these men. Poverty was considered a curse, a punishment for misbehavior. At first laziness or lack of planning and efficiency was the epitome of such misbehavior. Later, the cause for poverty was extended to include any sinfulness of the poor man. And still later—the book of Job was composed in the time of this transition—a man's poverty could be determined not only by his own sinfulness but by the wickedness of other men as well. The Old Testament has many passages in which the vices of the rich were blamed as the cause of the poverty of the poor. At this point in history, the concept of poverty has reached a crossroads. There is the way of the bitter, sour, despondent, desperate, cynical, greedy poor. It is a path without any future, a dead end. And there is the way of the poor who commit their cause to Yahweh. Through their suffering these people learn to trust in Yahweh in a special way. Their material needs bring home to them a profound sense of a far greater need for God: in every aspect of their existence they depend entirely on God. This second group of poor is called the "anawim"—the poor of Yahweh. In Psalm 73 we find a man fighting with himself to choose between these two paths. In the beginning of the psalm he is on the way of the "anawim," but soon he expresses jealousy and bitterness about the rich. Eventually, however, he returns to the fruitful spirituality of the "anawim" and to the complete peace that it offers. The "anawim" in their awareness of man's fundamental need for Yahweh were the open gate through which Yahweh's blessing and love entered into the people of Israel. They were a sacrament of Yahweh and a grace for the entire nation. In them the transition was made from poverty as a curse to poverty as a blessing. In them the miracle occurred that extraordinary weakness became a source of extraordinary strength, that is to say, their own weakness was empowered with Yahweh's strength. They were the humble, unobtrusive people without power or prestige, completely open to everything Yahweh could work in them and in their people. The "anawim" formed the minority who carried the Covenant and from whom Christ was born. Jesus belonged to this group and demanded of his disciples that they accept that same spirituality in practice as well as in spirit. St. Paul summarizes the life of Christ under the heading of poverty in this way: "Remember how generous the Lord Jesus was: he was rich, but he became poor for your sake, to make you rich out of his poverty" (2 Cor 8:9).

The biblical concept of poverty is related to but cannot be equated with the socio-economic poverty. It means far more than just the lack of material goods or of status. It is a positive ideal, the core of which is formed by a special attentiveness to God discovered in the painful reality of one's life experience. This openness to God carries with it an unusual degree of openness to men. Thus the poor man in the

113

evangelical sense is a man of distinctive character called "happy" by Christ in the first of his beatitudes. It is a grace and a blessing to be like this, worthy of divine congratulation.

According to human standards, the man who is poor in spirit is powerless, yet he is full of hope. He is simple and without pretentions. He may have possessions and talents, but he is not possessed by them. He doesn't have the mentality of ownership nor does he live under the delusion that a person *is* more when he *has* more. Paul's warning in his first letter to Timothy (6:17) is flesh and blood for him: "Warn those who are rich in this world's goods that they are not to look down on other people; and not to set their hopes on money, which is untrustworthy, but on God who, out of his riches, gives us all that we need for our happiness." Thus he has nothing to defend. He knows how to use the things of this world, how to give sincere attention to others without subordinating them to his own goals. He has the courage to make himself vulnerable as Jesus did. He does not cling to his time but makes himself available for those who need him. The man who is poor in spirit will approach the other person with an open heart, with his whole being and not just intellectually. He will give the other person time to say all that he has to say. He will be willing to share the other man's anguish, frustration, turmoil, limitations, guilt. Only then does the other man feel safe and at home. The man who is poor in spirit has a receptive mind and a hospitable heart. He is a master in the difficult art of listening. He has patience enough to allow the other person to discover for himself what the rich in spirit would love to teach him. He has respect for the sufferings of others and never even feels the temptation to think that he can remedy all situations. He convinces his fellowman that his doubts are taken seriously, that he is entitled to his questions, his problems, his mystery. Thus he never manipulates someone into an inferior position.

The man who is poor in spirit is not a scrupulously thrifty person as caricatures of poverty portray him, but he does have a deep and tender sensitivity for the material needs of individuals and nations. He may belong to that one-third of mankind for whom overweight and pollution are vital issues, but his concern reaches out to the undernourished and diseased of the other two-thirds of the family of man. "If a man who was rich enough in this world's goods saw that one of his brothers was in need, but closed his heart to him, how could the love of God be living in him?" (1 Jn 3:17) is his question just as much as it was John's. He knows that the new world to which he is dedicated is, in a very fundamental sense, not his own achievement but rather a gift to which he gives his time and talent. That new world is beyond him as is the kingdom of God, but that does not depress him or make him impatient and fanatical. He has assimilated the words of Christ: "There is no need to be afraid, little flock, for it has pleased your Father to give you the kingdom" (Lk 12:32). This gives him the courage to make a beginning, to be good not only in response to another's love but also to be good in response to another's need. Indeed, he shares in that divine quality of starting to love, to love first and thus always. That original and creative

115

aspect of God's love we find re-created in the poor in spirit. He realizes that he is a creature, that he is loved by God with a love which is based on nothing. "By loving us God makes us lovable" (St. Augustine) becomes a tangible reality in the heart of the poor man. Given to himself as a free gift from God, he is capable of accepting his own life in gratitude and, without clinging to it, passing it on to others.

In the man who is poor, there is never that self-complacency or narrow-mindedness which makes God superfluous. On the contrary, there is a constant awareness of his own insufficiency and weakness and need for God. This awareness is never disheartening. It is, rather, a great relief since it makes him rely not so much on his own strength but on God's. The realization that God is the main agent makes the burden light and the yoke easy and the heart still. Here we touch the heart of the poor man's mentality. Being ever-present to God who is Truth makes him poor in the deep and liberating sense of the word. He discovers that the most precious of all gifts is to disappear into the tremendous poverty which is the adoration of God (Thomas Merton). He has learned to stand before God with open hands, not clinging to anything. Even when the comfort and consolation of God's awareness in his prayer disappear, and when he feels stripped and naked in his presence, he doesn't complain. He waits not only for people but much more for God. The poor man is always a patient man. He has to wait so often in life. His emptiness before God is all right with him, too. He knows that it expresses a reality, and he has time and humility enough to endure until the Lord returns. In the meanwhile, he seeks no escape. He does not look for substitutes. He simply remains in the desert of his dryness without complaint. The stark faith-knowledge that he belongs to God and that God has hold of him even in the darkness is sufficient for the moment. In that desolate prayer, he knows himself to be in the good company of all men and women of prayer, of Christ himself.

Detachment from his experiences in prayer means a fortiori that the poor man is free in regard to the limitations of human life--his background, his health, his agedness, his inability to accomplish what he desires, his need for others. He has a self-image in which the awareness of these limitations is very vivid but it does not obsess or depress him. The consciousness of his own insufficiency without feelings of self-pity is typical of the poor in spirit. He realizes that he cannot love as much as his heart would wish. He faces the brevity of a good conversation as well as of a deep friendship. He accepts the barriers created by choices made in the past. The changes which he does not expect and which upset some of his peers, he takes graciously. He is not baffled when some cannot remain faithful to their original commitment in the midst of so much turmoil. He finds it hard enough himself. He is surprised by all the good he sees around him rather than scandalized by what he cannot judge anyway.

True poverty is not easy or cheap. In fact it can make life quite painful. But the man who is poor in spirit never yields to the temptation to nourish the pain, to indulge in self-pity, to foster feelings of inferiority. He is able to take all this in true self-acceptance without self-concern. He is not hard on himself nor does he wreak vengeance on himself. His self-acceptance is an act of faith. It is based on his belief that God accepts him as he is. That is why he can give himself to others wholeheartedly and yet remain himself. That is also why he always manages to be creative and optimistic in whatever life bestows on him, good or bad. He is grateful for his successes but not upset with his failures. He enjoys the good things but also admits the mistakes. There is a sense of humor in the midst of all his activities. He notices the little things without becoming petty and he faces his own defects which he has not yet overcome without becoming discouraged. The man who is poor in spirit is a contented person, happy and radiant without any superficiality.

This biblical poverty may be a lofty ideal. But is it realistic? No! For men this is impossible. For God, however, everything is possible (Mt 19:26). It is exactly the poor in spirit who is not turned off by this paradox but relieved and happy with it.

Fourteen

THE LEAST OF MY BROTHERS

At the Last Supper Jesus says, "My little children. . .I give you a new commandment: love one another; just as I have loved you, you also must love one another. By this love you have for one another everyone will know that you are my disciples" (Jn 13:34-35). Christ's legacy of love must be unique, something which has never been before; otherwise it would not be the distinguishing characteristic of Christians: "For I tell you, if your virtue goes no deeper than that of the scribes and the Pharisees, you will never get into the kingdom of heaven" (Mt 5:20).

We are told the revolutionary interpretation of love from Jesus himself. "There was a lawyer who, to disconcert him, stood up and said to him 'Master, what must I do to inherit eternal life?' He said to him, 'What is written in the law? What do you read there?' In reply, the scribe quoted two passages from Scripture. "He replied, 'You must love the Lord your God with all your heart, with all your soul, with all your strength, and with all your mind, and your neighbor as yourself' " (Lk 10:25 ff). The first part of this answer is no surprise to the Jews. It is the great commandment which every Jew recited before retiring at night and on rising in the morning.

119

> Listen, Israel: Yahweh our God is the one Yahweh. You shall love Yahweh your God with all your heart, with all your soul, with all your strength. Let these words I urge on you today be written on your heart. You shall repeat them to your children and say them over to them whether at rest in your house or walking abroad, at your lying down or at your rising; you shall fasten them on your hand as a sign and on your forehead as a circlet; you shall write them on the doorposts of your house and on your gates (Deut 6:4-9).

But it is strange for the scribe to quote Leviticus in the same breath: "You must love your neighbor as yourself" (19:18). How in the world can this man ferret out this tiny precept from all the minutiae of Leviticus and place it next to the great commandment of Deuteronomy? No Jew would ever do that! But Christ does it all the time. The lawyer, like the Pharisees, is annoyed with this rabbi who mixes the whole thing up by putting the commandment to love one another on the same level as the great commandment. This is heresy. He will clear this up once and for all. It is in order to incur an argument that he states Jesus' thesis to the crowd. Jesus does not wish a discussion. " 'You have answered right,' said Jesus, 'do this and life is yours.' But the man was anxious to justify himself, and said to Jesus, 'And who is my neighbor?' " The lawyer demands a definition of terms. This is natural to a lawyer at the beginning of a debate, but that he asks for a definition of "neighbor" indicates that he is outside the frame of the New Testament. To define means "to circumscribe, to set limits." Jesus refuses to define the term "neighbor" because by definition he would be excluding someone. But the scribe lives by definition. Indeed his whole existence is prescribed. He knows that there are six different explanations of the word "neighbor" according to six different schools of rabbis. The first says that a neighbor is a brother. The next says that neighbor includes friends also. The third school says that neighbor embraces the neighborhood, the village. The next school claims that neighbor is everyone who belongs to the Jewish race, the whole people. Another school says that not only those of the Jewish race but also those of the Jewish religion are to be loved. And the last school says that the term "neighbor" includes all those who are in the process of becoming Jews. There is one common element underlying the differing opinions and that is this: all draw a line somewhere, which is to say "Whoever is beyond this line, you may hate": "You have learned how it was said you must love your neighbor and hate your enemy" (Mt 5:43). The lawyer is actually asking Jesus "To which school do you belong?" "Which interpretation do you follow?" Jesus refrains from answering. Instead, he tells a story of a man who is on his way from Jerusalem to Jericho. Towards the end of the story, Jesus asks, "Which of these three, do you think, proved himself a neighbor to the man who fell into the brigands' hands?" This verse is the key to the whole parable because herein lies the doctrine. The question of the lawyer—Who is my neighbor?—is a self-centered question. It is a question of closed ethics. He is in the middle and there are circles around him which indicate the limits of his love. Christ preaches open ethics. He is saying that we must

121

identify neither with the one who comes to help nor with the one who refuses to help. Rather, we must place ourselves in the position of the person who needs help and then ask: "Who is my neighbor?" And we must do this every time. It is not we who are in the center but the one who needs help. So there is no end to the neighbor—open ethics. Everybody must be loved. There is no enemy. There is no limit to our charity. This is the revolution which Christ incited. No one had ever interpreted love this way:

> You have learnt how it was said: You must love your neighbor and hate your enemy. But I say this to you: love your enemies and pray for those who persecute you; in this way you will be sons of your Father in heaven, for he causes his sun to rise on bad men as well as good, and his rain to fall on honest and dishonest men alike. For if you love those who love you, what right have you to claim any credit? Even the tax collectors do as much, do they not? And if you save your greetings for your brothers, are you doing anything exceptional? Even the pagans do as much, do they not? (Mt 5:43-47).

Friendship is a rare gift of God. But friendship and love of neighbor are not identical. We miss the whole point of the New Testament if we reduce love of neighbor to friendship. Everybody has a few friends. There is nothing special about that. But Christ will not ask "Did you have many friends?" Christ will ask "Was there someone whom you rejected?" And if there is someone whom we reject, then our friendships are not Christian love. We may speak eloquently, prophesy the future of the world, the Church, the order, dedicate all we have and are to fight the poverty of this world, have a thousand friends, and in the eyes of Christ be without love.

The strongest indication of this unheard-of interpretation of love is found in the famous parable of the Last Judgment:

> "Then the virtuous will say to him in reply, 'Lord, when did we see you hungry and feed you. . .?' And the King will answer, 'I tell you solemnly, insofar as you did this to one of the least of these brothers of mine, you did it to me.'. . .Next he will say to those on his left hand, 'Go away from me, with your curse upon you. . .For I was hungry and you never gave me food;. . .Then it will be their turn to ask, 'Lord, when did we see you hungry or thirsty. . .and did not come to your help?' Then he will answer, 'I tell you solemnly, in so far as you neglected to do this to one of the least of these, you neglected to do it to me' " (Mt 25:37-45).

Strong as this language may be, we can even yet find a loophole. Who is the least? Is he the lowest on a list of important people—people ranked by their position? And is it what we do to this least—perhaps in our estimation the garbage collector or the janitor—that we do to Christ? Such an interpretation ridicules the Gospel. Christ has no list by title and precedence. There is, moreover, another list—and this list may be quite different from the first one!—which we all keep. This is our personal list of who comes first in our lives and who rates last. Christ identifies with these least of our brothers, these few whom we cannot stand. And what we do to these least we do to Christ. Whether we have been Christian or not, whether our lives have been worthwhile or fruitless, depends on our love for these least in our lives. Just as God accepts each of us, we, too, have to accept each of our brothers. This revolution, this Christian

123

love, is the agape which does not condemn our likes, our friendships, but goes beyond them:

> Agape does not deny the preferential love of the 'philia quality' (friendship), but it purifies it from a subpersonal bondage, and elevates the preferential love into a universal love. The preferences of friendship are not negated, but they do not exclude, in a kind of aristocratic self-separation, all the others. Not everybody is a friend, but everybody is affirmed as a person. Agape cuts through the separation of equals and unequals, of sympathy and antipathy, of friendship and indifference, of desire and disgust. It needs no sympathy in order to love; it loves what it has to reject in terms of 'philia'. Agape loves in everybody and through everybody love itself.[1]

Agape means that we love a person for what he is. Every person has an infinite mystery within himself. Agape penetrates this mystery to the deepest Ground. That is why the two commandments are equal. Suppose we know a person who lies ever so often. "We can prove it!" There is the possibility that we may see nothing else in him but liar. The Pharisees, in the same way, saw only the adulteress and nothing of the human personality, none of the circumstances. And that is a great sin against the first and second commandments. When we reduce a living person to the case of a liar, we negate God in that person. We deny that person his infinite depth, his deepest Ground. Agape means that we never confine the person to what we know of him:

> To love anyone is to hope in him for always. From the moment at which we begin to judge anyone, to limit our confidence in him, from the moment at which we

identify him with what we know of him and so reduce
him to that, we cease to love him and he ceases to be
able to become better. We should expect everything of
everyone. We must dare to be love in a world that does
not know how to love (Charles de Foucauld).

When we reduce persons whom we do not like to
something less than what they really are, there is a
danger that we reduce our friends, also, to something
very limited. The only difference is that we do not
mind their limitations. Then our friendships are
probably shallow. Abraham Lincoln once said, "I
don't like that man; I must get to know him." When
we do not like a person, we have not gone to the
depth of that person. This is Christian: to believe in
the good of every person. This is the revolution which
Christ taught.

"Love one another as I have loved you" (Jn
15:12). When we perceive what is said here, we feel
overcharged! To love as Christ loved! So many things
come to mind. Christ washed the feet of his disciples.
We cannot do that. He gave himself away in the
Eucharist as a little piece of bread and a sip of wine.
He cannot expect that of us. He prayed on the cross,
"Father, forgive them; they do not know what they
are doing" (Lk 23:34). We should take ridicule and
mockery, and then pray for our offenders? He called
Judas "friend" even as he received the kiss of
betrayal. We cannot say "friend" to one who betrays
us. He loved universally, accepted everyone. This is to
be admired, but we cannot imitate it. We can try, a
little bit, but not to the extent that Christ demands:
"Love one another as I have loved you." That is
impossible.

125

There are three ways out of this dilemma. First, we can say to ourselves "This Christ is too demanding" and seek out another religion. We reason that it is better not to be a Christian at all if it means being a half-hearted one. We had better give up now. The second way out is a little easier. In two minutes or less we can talk away the word "as" in the phrase "as I have loved you," and the problem along with it. We rationalize that we are stressing the word too much. We should at least take it in its broad, liberal sense and not confine the comparison. Under the guise of interpretation, we can dilute the words which make us feel uncomfortable. The third way out is the way of truth, namely, to give full weight to the word "as." The whole Gospel is summed up in that two-letter word "as." The Good News is this: know yourself loved by God. This is the content of our faith. If we allow this love to fill our hearts to the brim, it will overflow on to our neighbor. So then, the love of our neighbor is God's love. There is only one stream of love and it originates in God. He is the creative source of all love in this world. That love embraces us, takes us up and through us goes even further. Agape is a love which has discovered its source: "Love comes from God. . .God is love" (1 Jn 4:7,8). All the expertise of technology will not produce God. That is beyond our skill. And if we cannot produce God, we cannot produce Christian love either. Christian love is God himself or, in other words, sharing in that love which is God himself. We have only to open wide our hearts and love will flow in and through us to others. We are simply channels for his love. There is no strain to love. We are not

126

overcharged. On the contrary, we have been given an infinite treasure in God's love. It is gift. Faith, hope and charity are infused virtues. They are so tremendous that we can never achieve them. It is God himself: "This hope is not deceptive, because the love of God has been poured into our hearts by the Holy Spirit which has been given us" (Rom 5:5). The love of God has been poured into our hearts: "We can know that we are living in him and he is living in us because he lets us share his Spirit" (1 Jn 4:13). And the Jerusalem Bible adds this commentary: "It is God himself who through his spirit produces charity in us."

Now we understand why the least of our brothers is so important. God's love is universal. God's emeth never lets anybody down. The least of our brothers is the check as to whether our love is Christian love or a self-made product. The love of God has no limits. The theme of John's first letter is the intermingling of God's love for us and our love for our brother. He repeats this over and over again and still we manage to misunderstand and water-down the revolution of Christ. We mistakenly say "When we love each other, then God will come among us." But this is not what John is saying. This places the origin of love in ourselves. On these terms we have to fulfill a condition, and then God's love is ours. John says that God loves us first and the fruit, the result, of this love of God for us, is that we love one another. Our love for others is a continuation of God's love for us. John starts with God, not with ourselves or even with our love for others. He says the same in his Gospel (Chapter 15). The branch has to remain on the vine. The vine is the source of strength and love. This is where the love is at its fullest. The branch which remains on the vine will bear fruit and the only fruit that will remain—charity: "If you keep my commandments you will remain in my love. . . This is my commandment: love one another, as I have loved you" (Jn 15:10,12).

This Gospel is not depressing. It is truly Good News. It is not too demanding. So much is given to us that we are overwhelmed. How do we accept the least of our brothers? The answer is: not by will power but by opening ourselves to the love of God. There is only one way in which we can eventually accept everybody, even the difficult, impossible people. And that way is prayer. When we are on our knees, God will help us: "It is in deep solitude that I find the gentleness with which I can truly love my brothers. . . solitude and silence teach me to love my brothers for what they are, not for what they say" (Thomas Merton). In authentic prayer we come to the deepest Ground of their being. In authentic prayer we are filled so much with that love of God that we can accept even the least of our brothers. Christ came as a Savior and the greatest affliction he can save us from is the powerlessness to love. When Christ breaks down the barriers which we put up as limits to our love, then he is Savior. That is his mission. If only we let him do the work. If only we would not resist. And this is the meaning of prayer: that we open ourselves to the activity of the Father and of the Son and of the Holy Spirit.

Fifteen

PRAÜTES

"A single word characterizes the Jesus of the gospels and expresses his essential attitude to life: praütes. This word can only be translated very inaccurately into English." [1] When a word is typical for Jesus, it is worth a closer examination. When there is no accurate equivalent of this word in my own language, the investigation into the exact meaning of it is all the more pressing, for after all, "the limits of my language are the limits of my world" (Wittgenstein). In all scriptural references in this chapter the noun "praütes" or the adjective "praüs" occur in the Greek text. Together with the explanations given they may bring home to us the authentic meaning of the word in the New Testament, and thus help us to know Christ better.

To sense the meaning of "praütes" let us first look at the eight beatitudes not separately but as eight integrated statements, as an attempt to draw a self-portrait of Christ in eight strokes. Each line tries to express the same attitude from a different angle. Together they reflect the mentality of Jesus, his life-style, and of anyone who believes in him. The word "praütes" could serve as a summary of these eight beatitudes. The same is true of the fruits of the Spirit which Paul enumerates in Gal. 5:22: "What the Spirit brings is. . . love, joy, peace, patience, kindness, goodness, trustfulness, gentleness, and self-control." These, too, are not nine isolated qualities but rather nine expressions of the same Spirit which when combined portray a certain type of man, a true image of a Christian. Again, the word "praütes" stands as a synopsis of them all.

Since there isn't any English word which describes "praütes" accurately, there is a variety of translations. Sometimes translators will use the word meekness or gentleness or mildness. They also use the word peacefulness. Other translations are humility, unobtrusiveness, modesty, lowliness, calmness, or recollection. In classical Greek "praütes" is a word with a caress in it. The best translation may well be "with a still heart" which suggests the absence of turmoil. "Praütes" describes the person who radiates a still heart. It is something external—it can be detected in one's behavior—but its source is in the heart. It is an ideal to be realized insofar as the energies of the heart are attuned to it: "Do not dress up for show: doing up your hair, wearing gold bracelets and fine clothes; all this should be inside, in a person's heart, imperishable: the ornament of a sweet and gentle disposition (praüs)—this is what is precious in the sight of God" (1 Pet 3:3-4). St. Paul frequently uses the expression "clothe yourself with Christ" which amounts to "praütes."

Matthew's gospel account of Palm Sunday (21:5) visualizes "praütes" but we need a little background to relish this scene as an expression of it. The Romans ruled the world of their day and they knew that they must keep the people happy with bread and games. Ever so often they would sponsor a free festival for all the people of the city. An event which they regularly used for such a feast was the defeat of a foreign power. The general who had been in charge of the expedition would be given a tremendous reception on his return to Rome. The whole city would be involved in celebration for days.

Now, suppose a Roman soldier had witnessed such a demonstration. He saw all the wealth and luxury of the Roman empire bestowed · on that man as if he were a god. Suppose that same soldier happens to be in Jerusalem and he sees a man coming down from the Mount of Olives on his donkey with people shouting and waving branches from the trees. Then we know instinctively what "praütes" is in contrast to the Roman pageant. This man is humble, unobtrusive. He is a man with a still heart. We have to learn this, to train ourselves to it: "Learn from me for I am gentle and humble in heart, and you will find rest for your souls" (Mt 11:29). We find peace when we learn "praütes."

There is more to stillness than the silence of the tongue. There is, for instance, the silence of "we don't know what to say" like the vapid silence we call "angels passing by." Everyone is embarrassed, frantically searching for something to say. There is no stillness in anyone's heart! Silence can also be condemning. We can reprove a person without saying a word. When we do not speak to a person for a number of days, we hurt him more than words can do. That is not stillness, because our hearts are in turmoil. A story from Zen Buddhism gives us a good example of this. One day two monks set out on their journey to another monastery in a heavy downpour of rain. The road is quite muddy. All of a sudden, in the bend of the road, they see a beautiful young woman who is dressed in a silk kimono with a wide sash and carrying an umbrella to protect herself from the rain. And there she stands! Tanzan immediately understands. The girl wants to cross the road but she cannot because of the mud. Her dress will be stained. So Tanzan goes to the girl, picks her up in his arms, carries her over the muddy road, and puts her down. The two monks continue on their journey. Ekido doesn't say a word for the rest of the day. When they arrive at their destination, Ekido cannot restrain himself any longer. He says, "What you did was dangerous. Why did you do that? We monks stay away from women especially when they are young and pretty." And Tanzan replied, "I left that girl there. Do you still carry her?" Ekido's disturbance is not stillness of heart.

Guardini and others have stressed that silence and speech complement each other. We cannot speak if we are never silent; then we only rattle. On the other hand, silence which is not complemented by speech can be quite disconcerting. We can also say that silence and speech have a common root. There is one attitude which provides for both speech and silence, namely, the stillness of the heart. The silence of the mouth is only a prelude to this. The real stillness consists in the absence of self-concern. It is the peace of knowing oneself accepted by God as one is and abandoning oneself to his love. It is to rest secure with God in genuine closeness to him, surrendered to him without struggle or strain:

> Yahweh, my heart has no lofty ambitions,
>   my eyes do not look too high.
> I am not concerned with great affairs
>   or marvels beyond my scope.
> Enough for me to keep my soul tranquil and quiet
>   like a child in its mother's arms,
> as content as a child that has been weaned.

Israel, rely on Yahweh,
now and for always! (Psalm 131)

The Moslems say that two people have only learned to love each other when they can be silently together. In the beginning of their courtship, they have to talk incessantly and keep the conversation going so as not to embarrass one another. But as they grow in love they can be together for hours with hardly anything to say. Their very silence speaks of love. They know that the most essential realities are not expressed in words. The same holds true for our relationship with God. When we are really at home with him, we do not have to speak all the time. We can just be with him. This silent presence is rooted in stillness of heart—"praütes." From this stillness we can speak without breaking it: "Jesus came from silence. That was his home and he had to struggle to achieve speech. Man comes out of turmoil and noise, and silence is a task for him."[2]   From this silence we can say something which is worthwhile because in our silence we have more contact with people than we can ever have with speech alone. In that silence we can listen and then we can react and respond. "Praütes" brings thoughtfulness and wisdom, sensitiveness and sympathy to our words. It is said that the core of fanaticism is doubt. Fanatics are extremely outspoken because they have doubts in their hearts which they try to shout down. In the same sense we can say that the core of "praütes" is faith. Faith gives a relaxed attitude. We know ourselves loved by God and we are convinced of that. And in that faith we come to stillness and rest. And that is the beatitude of "praütes."

There is yet another way to grasp the meaning of "praütes." Many phrases in the Gospel such as "Be perfect as your heavenly Father is perfect" make impossible demands on us. This impossibility of the Gospel could crush us. But that is not the way of the Gospel! It makes demands which are utterly impossible for man. In fact, they are so impossible that we must change our attitude. We must come to realize that we can never make it, but that it is possible with God. So the impossibility of the Gospel should bring us to rely not on our own strength but on God's. And then it will give peace. When we try to do it ourselves, we will become downhearted and frustrated, or we will cut corners or make up our own anthology of the Gospel. These are ways out. If we take them, we make the most basic mistake we can possibly make. "Praütes" means to shoulder the Gospel the right way and to experience how light a burden it is, how graciously the Good News can be lived. The African woman who carries a heavy burden on her head can walk gracefully with it for miles if she balances it the right way. If she carries it the wrong way, she can hardly go fifty feet without straining her back. When we live the Gospel the right way, we are happy indeed. When we live it the wrong way, it is a terrible burden: "This is what loving God is—keeping his commandments; and his commandments are not difficult" (1 Jn 5:3). "Praütes" means that we focus on God. "Praütes" means that God is more important than ourselves. God has the initiative. "Praütes" means that passivity—what God does—is more important than activity—what we do. People with "praütes"

134

accomplish an unbelievable amount of work and, in addition, spend much time in prayer. How do they manage? Their hearts are still. They know themselves loved by God. There is no self-concern. Others squander the energies of their hearts. "Praütes" teaches us to get rid of the inner friction. We do not rely on our own achievements. What matters is that God loves us. When we place the emphasis on ourselves, we fail. The Gospel becomes impossible. There is another story from Zen Buddhism which tells of a bird lying on his back with his legs upward. Another bird comes along and says, "What's the matter with you? Why are you lying in a funny way like that?" "Oh," the bird answers, "I have to. I am holding up the sky. If I were to draw my legs back, the sky would fall and all the people would be killed." As it happened a leaf fell from a tree and came down with a rattling sound which frightened the bird. He turned over and flew away. The sky remained. When we, like the bird, consider ourselves as the center of the world, we cannot pray. Because God is no longer the focus, we lose the stillness of heart.

"Praütes" is not weakness or cowardice. What we may fail to realize is that "praütes" can only be possessed by a strong person. There is a gentleness in "praütes" but behind the gentleness there is the strength of steel. It is not a spineless gentleness, a sentimental fondness, a passive quietism. It is a strength which is under control—not so much self-control as God-control. The strength which is rooted in "praütes" is serene. Our petty faith is strained because we do not dare to surrender ourselves:

The early Christians realized the power of meekness, the sacred character and strength of defenselessness. A new force entered the world with the martyr who trembled, but stood firm, not revolting against anyone, and not debasing his suffering by ill-will or vanity. It is a great good fortune to meet a truly gentle person; it can mark a whole life.[3]

The person of "praütes" has hope. He is not pessimistic. He knows there is a future and he can explain why:

Simply reverence the Lord Christ in your hearts, and always have your answer ready for people who ask you the reason for the hope that you all have. But give it with courtesy and respect and with a clear conscience (1 Pet 3:15-16a).

This praütes renders his answer all the more effective:

If there are any wise and learned men among you, let them show it by their good lives, with humility and wisdom in their actions. . .The wisdom that comes down from above is essentially something pure; it also makes for peace, and is kindly and considerate; it is full of compassion and shows itself by doing good (James 3:13,17).

"Praütes" is more than a virtue. It is the summation of all the virtues of Christ. It gives us the attitude of Christ. It is untranslatable yet it can be expressed by our lives.

Sixteen

THE HOUR OF GLORY

"Now about eight days after this had been said, he took with him Peter and John and James and went up to the mountain to pray" (Lk 9:28 ff). While Jesus prays the reality of his Father's favor captivates him and radiates through him. His skin turns into light and his whole being is aglow. "As he prayed, the aspect of his face was changed and his clothing became brilliant as lightning. . .And a voice came from the cloud saying, 'This is my Son, the Chosen One. Listen to him.' "

All through the Old Testament the cloud is a symbol of God's presence. A cloud hovered over the ark. Mary was overshadowed by a cloud. Now a cloud envelops the disciples. They, too, are in the presence of God here on Mount Tabor. At the baptism Christ descended and put himself among sinners. At the transfiguration sinful man is lifted up to the mountain where God is present. The baptism of Christ and the transfiguration on Mount Tabor are turning points in the life of Christ. In the baptism the hidden life shifts to the public life. And the Father speaks at this decisive moment in the life of his Son. On Mount Tabor the public life moves into the passion. Again the Father speaks and expresses his pleasure with his Son: "This is my Son, the Chosen One." He is perfect. He fulfills the mission given him by his Father. "Listen to him." We never know Christ fully. We always remain disciples. And, if we should forget that our image and knowledge of Christ never do justice to the reality of the Person, then we will run into difficulties in our faith. We shall be disappointed and project our dissatisfaction onto him:

It was not any cleverly invented myths that we were repeating when we brought you the knowledge of the power and the coming of our Lord Jesus Christ; we had seen his majesty for ourselves. He was honoured and glorified by God the Father, when the Sublime Glory itself spoke to him and said, 'This is my Son, the Beloved; he enjoys my favour.' We heard this ourselves, spoken from heaven, when we were with him on the holy mountain. So we have confirmation of what was said in prophecies (2 Pet 1:16-19a).

The message of this mystery is that this glory comes from the cross. We find this interpretation in the patristic writings. The Fathers of the Church who preached often about the transfiguration always approached it as a preparation for the passion. The Eastern Church which still maintains August 6th as a solemn feast has the identical theme in her liturgy. And there are four other hints of this interpretation in the text of the Gospel itself. "Suddenly there were two men there talking with him; they were Moses and Elijah appearing in glory, and they were speaking of his passing which he was to accomplish in Jerusalem." The topic of conversation with Moses and Elijah is a strange one. This is the one day in the life of Christ that he is in his glory, and these two men speak of the passion and death which Jesus is to accomplish in Jerusalem. This seems a very inappropriate subject.

And yet, it is the obvious and proper topic for this occasion, for his glory which shines so brilliantly is the fruit of the passion. What is discussed and what is seen are related as cause and effect.

Why are Moses and Elijah the partners in this conversation? Presumably, because Moses as the lawgiver and Elijah as the greatest of the prophets together represent the Old Testament. There is more to it, however. Guardini explains that Moses had the thankless task to free his people from their shackles. Over a long period of time (40 years) he had to lead this stiff-necked people through all the hardship of the desert and to remain patient under all their resistance. And Elijah the Prophet struggled against the powers of evil during the reign of King Achab, the prototype of rebellion, and his terrible wife, Jezabel, more hardened in wickedness than he. All enmity against God, heritage of more than a thousand years of intractability and blindness, is carried between these two men.[1]

The third hint of this interpretation is found in the language of the gospels, especially the gospel of John. They use words which at first sight seem to have a double meaning, but for the person who believes the two meanings coincide. It is a gift of faith to see that the two realities are basically one and the same. We can consider the phrase "the hour." We imagine "the hour" as the most successful moment in a person's life, the peak of his career. For Christ, "the hour" is Calvary. Herein is the double meaning. We think "the hour" as glory but the glory is in the cross. The word "glorified" is another example. At first glance we think of "glorified" as exuberant praise, ecstatic applause. For Christ, the crucifixion is the hour of glorifications:

> Now the hour has come
> for the Son of Man to be glorified.
> I tell you, most solemnly,
> unless a wheat grain falls on the ground and dies,
> it remains only a single grain;
> but if it dies,
> it yields a rich harvest (Jn 12:23-24).

The glorification and the crucifixion blend. They are two sides of the one coin. We cannot separate them. That is the mystery of Mount Tabor.

The fourth intimation is the setting of the episode of the transfiguration within the framework of the gospels. All three synoptic gospels have the same structure: 1) the profession of faith by Peter: "You are the Christ, the Son of the living God." Immediately following this is 2) the first prophecy of the passion. The disciples are considered strong enough to hear of Christ's death. But the trust proves premature. Peter remonstrates: "Heaven preserve you, Lord; this must not happen to you" (Mt 16:22). Then 3) the event of the transfiguration is related—another attempt to convey the same message. Now Christ tries not in word but in mystery to impress upon the disciples that same prophecy of the suffering servant. After that comes 4) the second prophecy of the passion in words. The transfiguration is set between the two prophecies of the passion. That is sufficient to indicate that it is a prophecy in itself.

The confession of Peter, the two prophecies of the passion, and the transfiguration are inseparable.

We can say that the transfiguration is an object lesson in the theology of the cross which is the most difficult chapter in theology to understand then and now. Christ with all his teaching ability failed to communicate the lesson of the cross. Even after his death and resurrection he had to give private lessons on the subject! To the disciples of Emmaus he had to say: "Did not the Messiah have to undergo all this so to enter into his glory?" (Lk 24:26 NAB). They could not grasp his reasoning!

We will all have to face the cross one day. It will come in a way which we least expect. No matter how blessed we are with imaginative powers, we simply will not discover what cross is in store for us. We would do better to look upon the glory of Christ in the transfiguration and try to understand its source, to grasp its relation to the cross. Then, when the cross comes into our lives no matter how unexpected, we may recognize and be ready for it. And that is enough. It is a pity when people who have meditated much on the Gospel do not identify the cross when it comes as the cross of Christ. Instead, they become rebellious, bitter and self-indulgent. They miss the chance of their lives. The moment of glory came and they let it go by. They were not prepared for the cross. Now all this—true as it may be—should not lead us to an unhealthy mystique of suffering which tries to find "crosses" everywhere and manages to find them, too! Let us rather be realistic and face the fact that part of our trouble is unreal:

> Most of us suffer distress not in the fact that realities which truly matter go awry but in the frustrations of

141

artificial goals, conventional values, arbitrary objectives. Human life is under siege not because so many important things go wrong but because men make lesser values the standard of what human life must become. This is not to dismiss tragedy, but it is to put things into perspective.[2]

Sometimes we are trapped in needless worry. We can suffer from that but we should not and we need not. It is a pity. There is so much genuine misery in the world that it is a waste to suffer under things which are not sufferings at all.

The genuine life-style of the Gospel will bring deep peace and fulfillment but only through the emptying of oneself, as it was with Jesus himself. His way of life was extraordinarily fruitful but at the cost of deep-felt kenosis. He belonged to the people and was their property. He did not manipulate them or enjoy himself at their expense or behave pompously among them. On the contrary, he let the need of the people flow into his heart and shared it with them. No one was unimportant in his eyes, no one was ever considered a hopeless case. This required a true unselfishness. The obscurity of Jesus' life-style was essential to his goodness. It is precisely his deep humility which enabled him to be so fruitful for many:

Humility comes from the Latin word "humus", fertile ground. The fertile ground is there, unnoticed, taken for granted, always there to be trodden upon. It is silent, inconspicuous, dark; and yet it is always ready to receive any seed, ready to give it substance and life. The more lowly, the more fruitful, because it becomes really fertile when it accepts all the refuse of the earth. It is so low that nothing can soil it, abase it, humiliate it; it has accepted the last place and cannot go any lower.[3]

This secret of the Master is also the secret of his followers. In the Christian humility their lives will become wonderfully fertile and show the glory of the kenosis.

Simone Weil remarked that the extraordinary greatness of Christianity is not that it provides us with medicine against suffering, but that it gives perspective to suffering. Christianity does not spare us pain. The Gospel does not promise that we will not suffer. Indeed, the Gospel makes it very clear that we do have to lose our lives, to take up our cross and follow Christ. And that is unique! All other religions either try to avoid pain or make one immune to it so that it will no longer be felt. This is not the Gospel approach. The cross remains a human reality but the Gospel gives meaning to it, and that fact makes the difference. Once we know that suffering has a purpose, or at least once we can believe that there is a meaning to it, we can endure much more. That is the Gospel message—that suffering need not be a loss. People can grow bitter through suffering but they can also become beautiful. And the latter serve as a grace to others. Their suffering has made them transparent, more open, wise and gentle. In them, we see the fruitfulness of the cross. Pain can glorify us, make us radiant and give a fruitfulness to our lives:

God lets himself be pushed out of the world on to the cross. He is weak and powerless in the world, and that is precisely the way, the only way, in which he is with us and helps us. Matt 8:17 makes it quite clear that Christ

helps us, not by virtue of his omnipotence, but by virtue of his weakness and suffering.
Here is the decisive difference between Christianity and all religions. Man's religiosity makes him look in his distress to the power of God in the world: God is the 'deus ex machina.' The Bible directs man to God's powerlessness and suffering; only the suffering God can help.[4]

Christ on the cross alone can give meaning to our suffering. And isn't that true? Millions of simple people have found the strength to bear suffering because they held the crucifix in their hands. That is Christianity. Pagan theology says "If you are the Son of God, come down from the cross." The Gospel says, "Because I am the Son of God, I remain on the cross." That is the message of the transfiguration. There we see the glory of the cross. There is no other way to be so radiant, to spread so much light in this world but through the cross.

Seventeen

HE EMPTIED HIMSELF

Jesus sent Peter and John from Bethany to Jerusalem to make the preparations for the feast of the Passover. A few hours later, Jesus arrived with the other ten of the disciples. It will be the last evening that Jesus is to be alive and he wants to spend it with his disciples: "It has been my heart's desire. I have longed and longed for this evening." He would like to draw some courage, some comfort and strength from being together with his friends before the Passion begins. He has also longed for this meal to share a most precious gift with his disciples. He is going to give himself away. He will hand himself out as a little piece of bread so small and insignificant. So much will he empty himself. The Last Supper is a mystery of the emptying of Christ.

"A dispute arose also between them about which should be reckoned the greatest" (Lk 22:24). The feast of feasts which Christ had anticipated for so long begins with a quarrel, an ugly quarrel about something so alien to his mentality: "which should be reckoned the greatest." The last day of his life, and his friends fight for the first place. Most quarrels are exactly this. No matter how well we hide behind theological or sociological masks, the real issue is usually that we believe that we are greater and we are not going to yield. How many times had Christ put a child in their midst? They haven't yet begun to grasp the message. This evening is a tremendous disappointment to Christ. His own disciples give him the feeling that his whole life has been a failure. He had never succeeded with the leaders of the people; they had rejected him from the very beginning. For a time he was popular with the people but then gradually he lost them, too. On Palm Sunday there was a terrific demonstration of enthusiasm but tomorrow they will cry just as loudly: "Crucify him." And now his disciples make abundantly clear this very hour that they, too, have missed the whole point of his message. They are no better than the others. They want to be so important! He has achieved nothing, and tomorrow everything will be finished.

Each of us, sooner or later, will face a situation which at least from a distance can be compared to this moment. We will feel as Christ felt during the Last Supper.

— It may be the death of someone very dear to us, an agonizing death which is unbearable to witness. And we ask "How can God permit this?"

— Or the moment may come when a friend whom we love, to whom we have confided our deepest thoughts and ideals, turns and goes another way. We feel betrayed. It is not our enemies who make us suffer most but our friends, people whom we love. Only they can make us suffer. That can cause a crisis similar to the one Christ suffered here. He had shared everything with these men, and they betrayed him right in the heart of his message.

– Or we may be disappointed in ourselves. All of a sudden we see such a gap between what we say and what we are that we become paralyzed. We would even like to run away from our commitment, from the whole Gospel, because we feel we are frauds. All of life is one big lie.

– Or there is the crisis of being told that everything we have labored for was done the wrong way. It is all a failure. Things have changed now and there is little that we have contributed after all.

– Perhaps we say to ourselves "It would be better if we had not been born."

A curse on the day when I was born,
no blessing on the day my mother bore me!
A curse on the man who brought my father the news,
'A son, a boy has been born to you!'
making him overjoyed.
May this man be like the towns
that Yahweh overthrew without mercy;
may he hear alarms in the morning,
the war cry in broad daylight,
since he did not kill me in the womb;
my mother would have been my tomb
while her womb was swollen with me.
Why ever did I come out of the womb
to live in toil and sorrow
and to end my days in shame! (Jer 20:14-18)

In such a crisis, Christ still has something to say. The profession of faith in the early Church was very brief—"Jesus is Lord." This means among many other things that Christ can cope with any situation. He can handle this crisis, too. But, whereas we are tempted to make a scene and to put people in their place, Christ shows us another way. He goes one step further in his humiliation. He gives us a good example of what he said in the Sermon on the Mount:

> You have learnt how it was said: Eye for eye and tooth for tooth. But I say this to you: offer the wicked man no resistance. On the contrary, if anyone hits you on the right cheek, offer him the other as well; if a man takes you to law and would have your tunic, let him have your cloak as well. And if anyone orders you to go one mile, go two miles with him. Give to anyone who asks, and if anyone wants to borrow, do not turn away (Mt 5:38-42).

His disciples humiliate him. And Jesus humbles himself even more. That is *his* solution. When our sorrow overwhelms us, we can either take refuge in self-pity, escape into substitutes or we can surrender ourselves, forget about ourselves, empty ourselves. This is a moment of grace in which all of life pushes us to greater abandonment: who loses his soul will find it. This is the moment when it is most easy to lose ourselves. And in giving up ourselves, in letting go of that last little bit of ourselves, we find a new dimension to our faith.

Christ now enters the second stage of his emptying. He washes the feet of his disciples. We will never be able to understand what this really means. It is something foreign to our culture. What does it mean to be a slave? What does it mean to wash someone's feet? The apostles were staggered at the thought. They had no specific objections. They did not even think of excuses for Jesus. What they wanted to say—"You can't do this! You're throwing

your life away!"—they couldn't. The dismay of the
apostles! This is the heroism of the Gospel: to wash
someone else's feet. The sons of thunder, James and
John, had wanted to call down fire from heaven
because the message of the Gospel was not received
immediately. They were also the ones who came with
their mother to ask secretly for the first places in the
kingdom of heaven. Now Christ says that if they want
the first place, they must wash the feet of their
fellowman. The tax collector, Matthew, had been
rich. How often had his slaves, at his slightest gesture,
knelt down and washed his feet. Tonight it is the
Master who kneels. And then there is Judas who is
full of deception, ready to betray his Master, but
Christ does not pass him up. That would be closed
ethics. He washes the feet of the man who in a matter
of hours will deliver him with a kiss. That is Christ.
He emptied himself. This humility is part of Christian
love. Christian love is unique. It is different from all
other types of love. What calls itself "love" is at times
mainly the desire for possession of the other person,
and what considers itself service and availability can,
in fact, be quite selfish. There is the temptation to
make use of other people for one's own image.
Christian love has humility at its roots. It requires
tremendous generosity and a constant battle with
one's own egoism and desire for self-assertion to
maintain the attitude of Christian love. Anyone who
lives by Christian love will reach a juncture in his life
where he meets the challenge to enter into genuine
humility. And if he refuses to do that, then his
Christian love dies or turns into a caricature of love.
It is the tragedy of human life that selfishness always

creeps into our generosity and dedication. When, in our service to others, our own importance grows and we become more domineering, there is something wrong. We can love people and work hard and yet seek ourselves at the same time. It is Christian love and service to wash each other's feet, to look for the last place.

Christ wants to be with us. He wants to give himself to us completely. In the third stage of emptying, Christ made himself into a small piece of bread and a little wine: "For my flesh is real food and my blood is real drink. He who eats my flesh and drinks my blood lives in me and I live in him" (Jn 6:55-56). We know that a gift is more precious when the giver puts more of himself into it. It then becomes more valuable as a gift. Christ's gift is invaluable for he put his whole self into his gift. Gift and Giver are identical. This we can never do. On the other hand, to receive a gift requires a certain amount of simplicity. We need only be grateful! When we analyze a gift, we make it into a problem. A gift on that level is impossible. A gift is always on the level of mystery. Some people just cannot accept mysteries. Whatever they receive has to be analyzed and solved. There are no gifts in their lives. So, too, they must pull the Eucharist apart until there is no gift left. To meet Christ in the Eucharist we must make ourselves small. If we cannot kneel, if we cannot wash the feet of our fellow man, then we cannot believe in the Eucharist. It is the mystery in which Christ empties himself. It is a symbol, but a sacramental symbol. And a sacrament is a very special kind of symbol which realizes what it expresses in the symbol. It is the body of Christ. To try to explain it is already to have lost it. We receive it as Gift. People who want to be important should ask themselves, "What does Christ do in the Eucharist?"

The main dish of the Last Supper was the one-year-old lamb which Peter and John had gone on ahead to prepare. For the apostles, this lamb was a reminder of the past. The passover lamb was the memorial of the exodus from Egypt, and all the powerful miracles that went with it as unequivocal signs of Yahweh's faithfulness to his Chosen People. For Christ, however, this lamb was a sign which pointed into the very near future. Tomorrow, Christ will be the lamb led to the slaughter house. Leviticus (16:20-22) narrates the ritual of the scapegoat which was loaded with the sins of Israel and then led into the desert. Tomorrow, Christ will be the lamb of God who takes away the sins of the world (Jn 1:29) by carrying the terrible load on his shoulders and out of this world. Every year the high priest would go into the sanctuary to sprinkle the ark of the covenant with "blood that was not his own" (Heb 9:25). Tomorrow Christ will enter the sanctuary once and for all "taking with him his own blood" (Heb 9:12). For Christ, the Last Supper is the limit of self-emptying. He knows full well that when he breaks the bread, he is breaking his own body. The die is cast. The ritual of the Last Supper will have to be completed the next day in all of its cruel reality. Christ initiates this himself: "No one takes my life from me; I lay it down of my own free will" (Jn 10:18). St. Paul tells us that "every time we eat this bread and drink this cup we are proclaiming his death" (1 Cor 11:26). This is all the more true of the One eating of the

151

bread and drinking of the cup *before* Good Friday. At the Last Supper, too, the death of Christ was proclaimed, called down by the One who realized the full impact of what he was doing at this meal. Here the kenosis of Christ reached its depth since it implied his whole passion and death. The glory and the fruitfulness of this emptying-out of Christ we celebrate in every Eucharist. The bread that is broken nourishes the life of Christ in us until he comes.

Eighteen

THE PRAYER OF A POOR MAN

"After singing songs of praise they left for the Mount of Olives" (Mk 14:26 NAB). That the Last Supper ends with songs of praise is due to Christ. If Christ had not humbled himself, then the Last Supper which began with a quarrel would not have ended with a hymn. Jesus leads the disciples to the place where he usually spent his nights: "In the daytime he would be in the Temple teaching, but would spend the night on the hill called the Mount of Olives" (Lk 21:37). He courageously walks towards danger not away from it: "No one takes my life from me; I lay it down of my own free will" (Jn 10:18). He leaves eight of the disciples at the entrance to the estate. They have to think things out among themselves. So much has happened in so short a time! Jesus takes with him Peter, James and John—the three apostles who on Mount Tabor had glimpsed the glory that comes from the cross. These three, Jesus believes, are best prepared to be with him in this moment of anguish. But he is mistaken.

"And a sudden fear came over him and great distress" (Mk 14:34). As he approaches Gethsemane, a tremendous change comes over him. It is as if he were another person. Christ had always known about his passion. He knew by heart the prophecies and psalms which foretell the sufferings the Messiah would undergo. He himself had mentioned his passion several times: "There is a baptism I must still receive, and how great is my distress till it is over" (Lk 12:50). He had no fear then. Not too long ago he had resolutely traveled the road to Jerusalem (Lk 9:51) which was a hot-bed of Pharisees. Jerusalem promised nothing but peril for him. In going, he ran the risk—life itself, but from this he did not shrink. On another occasion, when he received word that his friend Lazarus was ill, he said to his disciples " 'Let us go to Judea.' The disciples said, 'Rabbi, it is not long since the Jews wanted to stone you; are you going back again?' " The disciples were so convinced that his going to Jerusalem was going to his death that "Thomas—known as the Twin—said to the other disciples, 'Let us go, too, and die with him' " (Jn 11:7-8,16). But now in Gethsemane, Jesus is filled with fear and anguish. There is a difference between knowing something remotely and knowing the same thing close at hand. We know, for instance, that one day we shall die. But when a doctor says, "You have one month to live," our perspective of death changes. This very night the passion of Christ will begin, and tomorrow it will all be over.

If we approach the agony reverently, we see its three-fold dimension predicted in three verses of the Deutero-Isaiah: 1) "Yahweh has been pleased to crush him with suffering" (Is 53:10). Christ foresees his whole passion and many details of the sufferings that lie ahead for him. The first way of the cross was made by Christ in Gethsemane. And as he pauses at each station, he becomes more and more afraid. He doesn't know where to go, so much does the anguish grip him. He sees so much pain, so much cruelty. It is unbearable for a human being, and Christ is human.

The Prayer of a Poor Man

Yet here am I, now more worm than man,
scorn of mankind, jest of the people,
all who see me jeer at me,
they toss their heads and sneer,
'He relied on Yahweh, let Yahweh save him!'

A herd of bulls surrounds me,
strong bulls of Bashan close in on me;
their jaws are agape for me,
like lions tearing and roaring.

I am like water draining away,
my bones are all disjointed,
my heart is like wax,
melting inside me;
my palate is drier than a potsherd
and my tongue is stuck to my jaw.

A pack of dogs surrounds me
a gang of villains closes me in;
they tie me hand and foot
and leave me lying in the dust of death.

I can count every one of my bones,
and there they glare at me, gloating;
they divide my garments among them
and cast lots for my clothes (Psalm 22:6-8,12-18).

2) The pain of suffering is great but added to this
is the far greater burden of our sins: "We had all gone
astray like sheep, each taking his own way, and Yahweh
burdened him with the sins of all of us" (Is 53:6). The
sins of the whole world are placed on his shoulders and
the load is a heavy one. He just cannot bear it. He
breaks down. The feeling of guilt is a terrible
suffering, the worst suffering in the world. Think of
the person who has killed a child through an

155

unfortunate car accident; he will never forget it. Christ is burdened with the guilt of mankind, not just the guilt from accidents or mistakes, but the whole gamut of ways in which people do harm to people. Christ has always known that he was in the favor of the Father. In fact, that was the secret of his life. Now he knows that he is sin, just sin: "for our sake God made the sinless one into sin" (2 Cor 5:21). What started at his baptism has now become the full reality. Then Christ shared our sinfulness. Now he *is* sin. How he suffers! He is like a leper, or worse. We can commit sin. That is easy enough. But we can never fathom the depth of our sinfulness. Sin is always greater than what we can grasp or comprehend. Only Christ can measure it and plumb its very depth. Pascal once said, "You'll get to know sin to the degree that you expiate it." That is why we know so little about sin. Christ in Gethsemane knows precisely what sin is. Everything becomes transparent—every thought, every action. He sees beneath the apparent beauty to the sinfulness, the selfishness, the pride. It is no longer hidden. Christ is surrounded by sin. He has become sin itself. And this is real, not a substitute. We cannot say that Christ merely suffered vicariously. This is to admit that we do not know what love is. When we really love a person, we experience the guilt of that person as our very own guilt. That is the secret of love as parents well know. Christ had enough love for each of us to really take our guilt, and experience it as his own. It is not "as if;" it is sheer reality. In the full sense of the word, Christ became sin.

3) As the relative uselessness of the passion dawns upon Christ, his anguish is intensified: "I was

thinking I have toiled in vain, I have exhausted myself for nothing" (Is 49:4). Christ sees in Gethsemane the sins of the people who know of his passion, who have prayed about it, yet who still compromise their lives. His passion doesn't make much of a difference to them. It doesn't change their world. These, his friends, make the most terrible contribution to his suffering:

> Were it an enemy who insulted me,
> I could put up with that;
> had a rival got the better of me,
> I could hide from him.
>
> But you, a man of my own rank,
> a colleague and a friend,
> to whom sweet conversation
> bound me in the house of God! (Ps 55:12-14).

Jesus suffers from the thought that his passion might be a waste, that people still will not understand:

> I know all about you: how you are neither cold nor hot. I wish you were one or the other, but since you are neither, but only lukewarm, I will spit you out of my mouth (Revel 3:15-16).

The mediocrity of our lives must disappoint him. We are afraid to allow the passion to touch us, afraid to go too deep for fear it may change our lives. Christ realizes that and he is in anguish and distress. Up until now he had been so eager to begin the work of redemption. Now there is only revulsion: "For it is not as if we had a high priest who was incapable of feeling our weaknesses with us; but we have one who has been tempted in every way that we are; though he is without sin" (Heb 4:15). It is a terrible temptation for Christ to limit himself to "common sense." If his passion will not mean much to the world, then why go through this suffering of pain and guilt? In our lives, too, the worst temptation is not the temptation to commit a particular sin like stealing or murder, but the temptation to deny God, to say that he doesn't exist, to say that he is merely a projection of a need, to confine ourselves to a pagan existence. This is the basic temptation. In forgetting that there is a God, we can take control of our own lives. We can be like God. Christ overcomes the temptation in prayer, the prayer of petition: "Abba (Father)!" he said, "Everything is possible for you. Take this cup away from me. But let it be as you, not I, would have it" (Mk 14:36). This prayer has no flowery utterances. It is just a simple prayer which Christ repeats over and over, fighting and struggling all the while. This prayer transforms his attitude. He overcomes his revulsion. At the end, when the soldiers come, he is ready: "The hour has come. Now the Son of Man is to be betrayed into the hands of sinners. Get up! Let us go! My betrayer is close at hand already" (Mk 14:42). Several times Jesus comes to the disciples, newly ordained priests, for help. He doesn't ask that they draw a sword. He only asks that they watch one hour with him. But they let him down. They love Christ, but not enough to do the little things he asks:

> Look on my right and see,
> there is no one to befriend me,

All help is denied me,
no one cares about me (Ps 142:4).

A stone's throw away they sleep, and Christ remains in utter distress. The disciples do not realize that Christ is suffering. How often this is true. Sometimes at a short distance someone can be in distress, and we do not know it. And that is our sin: "We didn't know it." From this sin Christ had to suffer. He asked them to stay one hour with him in his agony, an unheard-of invitation. We are invited to come and share the sufferings of our God. It is the wisdom of the cross that in this suffering man can meet God himself. That is where God is found. All through the centuries people have found in the suffering Lord the strength to bear their sufferings, their cross.

Nineteen

HIS LOVE IS EVERLASTING

The word "resurrection" is like an ocean. It has an infinite beauty. We cannot grasp it; it slips like water through our fingers. Nor can we see beyond its horizon. It is also dangerous. We can easily drown in it. Again, the word "resurrection" is like the Grand Canyon. Its awesome grandeur we can never fully explore. And there is the risk that we get lost in it.

The mystery of the Resurrection is not as easy for us to accept as it used to be some decades ago. Is it a body formed from a corpse? How does that work? Is it a body which is agile, penetrable, radiant? How do we imagine something like that? Is it an immediate physical and spiritual communion with the universe so that the earth becomes a part of the structure of our body-soul unity? St. Paul was asked similar questions regarding it: "Someone may ask 'How are dead people raised, and what sort of body do they have when they come back?' " (1 Cor 15:35). His answer is sharp: "These are stupid questions!" Why? They turn the mystery into a problem: "We teach what scripture calls: the things that no eye has seen and no ear has heard, things beyond the mind of man, all that God has prepared for those who love him" (1 Cor 2:9). And whatever answer *we* give is within the mind of man and, therefore, cannot be correct. The resurrection is a

161

mystery in the full sense of the word. We believe in it, but we cannot explain exactly what we believe. It is a mystery we have to learn to live with. There is a folly of the cross, and there is a folly of the resurrection, too. St. Paul experienced this in Athens as we read in Acts 17. Athens was the intellectual center of the world of his day. Rome might have had the military and political power but Athens had the long-standing tradition of the brains and the culture. The Athenian supreme council gathered at the Areopagus, and Paul's speech there was the highlight of his apostolic career. It was a well-prepared discourse, starting with an exordium worthy of his sophisticated audience. After a while, Paul introduced the subject of the resurrection: " 'And God has publicly proved this by raising this man from the dead.' At this mention of rising from the dead, some of them burst out laughing; others said 'We would like to hear you talk about this again.' After that Paul left them. . ." (31-33). It was without a doubt a most frustrating end to a once-in-a-lifetime chance. And yet, the fiasco of the Areopagus was by no means Paul's most painful experience of the folly of the resurrection. Later, Paul was put on trial which lasted for years and ended in his death sentence. Paul was convinced that the resurrection was the real issue in this court case: "It is for our hope in the resurrection of the dead that I am on trial" (Acts 23:6). It will do us no harm to experience some embarrassment for the sake of the resurrection once in a while. It will put us in good company.

For some people the folly of the resurrection is more than they can take. It gives them a downright inferiority complex in the living of their faith. Consequently, they feel tempted to dilute the mystery of the resurrection to such an extent that it can be accepted by everybody. The worst thing about an inferiority complex is that it inevitably turns into its reverse. People with an inferiority complex sooner or later assume a superior behavior. Some will control another person by leaning heavily and constantly on him. Others will almost always in a kind of lame, depressive mood withdraw themselves, but on rare occasions they will come out of their corner to say or do things which no one else would have the nerve to do. People whose faith suffers from an inferiority complex, alas, manifest that same tendency to manipulate other people, this time in matters of faith. They can have a disruptive influence and form the breed from which heresy hunters come. Their intransigence masks an uncomfortableness with the mystery which cannot be explained. To live with a mystery requires a certain amount of humility.

If we cannot say what resurrection is, then let us at least say what it is not! In the first place, the resurrection is not just to say that Christ lives on in our memory, that his words are still alive among us, and that his name will never pass out of this world. This is too meager, for in that case resurrection would be a very common phenomenon. The many words and famous names of Shakespeare, Plato, David and a host of others are still among us. This interpretation makes resurrection so general that it no longer has a special meaning. There is a second and more serious reason why this explanation is too meager. It purports that Christ lives among us because we are still talking about him. He owes his resurrection to us. He lives, thanks to us. This is a precise reversal of Scripture which has us live, thanks to him: ". . .God sent into the world his only Son so that we could have life through him" (1 Jn 4:9). The basic fallacy here is that we make ourselves the origin and foundation of the resurrection, whereas Christ "should be first in every way" (Col 1:18).

A second insufficient interpretation of the resurrection is more subtle. According to this theory, resurrection signifies that one is able to live with death staring in one's face and yet be happy. Heaven means the acceptance of the idea that there is no heaven. Once we are courageous enough to give up our childhood faith, which postpones happiness till after death and frightens us with the terror of hell, we reach happiness and freedom here on earth—and that is heaven. This explanation falls short exactly because it is so clear. An I.Q. of 110 will do to understand this theory completely. That is to say, that there is no mystery left. The "unknown" of the resurrection is turned into a problem, which then is effectively solved. And thus the enigma is explained away. St. Paul had something more in mind when he wrote "If there is no resurrection of the dead, Christ himself cannot have been raised, and if Christ has not been raised then our preaching is useless and your believing it is useless;. . .For if the dead are not raised, Christ has not been raised, and if Christ has not been raised, you are still in your sins. . .If our hope in Christ has been for this life only, we are the most unfortunate of all people (1 Cor 15:14,17,19).

A third false understanding of the resurrection is to see it as a return from death to life. Lazarus, the youth of Nain, the daughter of Jairus returned from death. Christ did not. There is an essential difference between these three people and Jesus. This leads us to the correct answer concerning the nature of the resurrection. After the three negative enunciations we shall make two positive statements about what resurrection truly is.

Resurrection, then, is not a return from death but a break through death into a life in which death has no power anymore: "Christ, as we know, having been raised from the dead will never die again. Death has no power over him any more" (Rom 6:9). This is the basic difference between Lazarus and Christ. Lazarus returned to life and then he had to die again. Christ did not return to this life but he has broken through death into a new life. There is no death ahead of him any more. And that is the definition of the resurrection: life over which death has no power. When we say this, we say the precise truth but as we do so, we do not know what we mouth! With words we articulate a mystery. Though we express it in words, it still remains a mystery. Biology says a great deal about life—life with death in it. Life without death is beyond our knowledge. The most simple person knows that life ends in death. This doesn't hold for Christ any more. Our life experience is the mixture of life and death together. What life itself is, we do not know. What we call life isn't life, really. People over thirty years of age who can no longer do what they were capable of doing when they were younger can feel how death is at work in their bodies. Eventually, death will win. It will destroy the body and, finally, life itself. We shall all die. We call this life, but death is involved in it; death has power over it. Christ lives a life over which death has no power whatsoever. That is real life. That is pure life, a life beyond our grasp.

The early Church proclaimed her faith in a formula of two words—"Kyrios Jesus"—Jesus is Lord. For the early Christian this proclamation meant "Jesus is lord of my life." It implied a personal relationship with Christ, in which he abandoned himself completely to the Lord. There is adoration in it. The formula also means that Jesus is Lord over every power in this world. There are no restrictions. Every power on this earth is transcended by Jesus. What is the greatest power in this world? Death. A politician may be very powerful, but one day he will die. An athlete may be very strong but one day death will be stronger. "Jesus is Lord" means that Christ has overcome that power: "and the last of the enemies to be destroyed is death, for everything is to be put under his feet" (1 Cor 15:26). "Jesus is Lord" because he is raised from the dead. In a verse which is abundantly clear because of the parallelism which says things twice St. Paul states: "If your lips confess that Jesus is Lord and if you believe in your heart that God raised him from the dead, then you will be saved" (Rom 10:9). "If your lips confess" is synonymous with "if you believe in your heart;" and "Jesus is Lord" is equivalent to "God raised him from the dead." The corresponding formula is "Christ Jesus." Christ means "the anointed one," "the

Messiah." When we can identify Jesus of Nazareth, the carpenter-Rabbi who died on a cross, with Christ the Lord, then we believe.

The mystery of the resurrection is central to our faith. If Christ is not risen, then our faith collapses. Nothing remains. The Gospel should be read from the viewpoint of the resurrection because that is the way it was written. Every episode of the Gospel is imbued with the light of the resurrection. When we take the resurrection out, there is nothing left to the Gospel, just as when we take the head from the body the rest becomes a corpse. When we leave out the resurrection, we cannot use anything from the Gospel, because the core of the Gospel is the resurrection. This is what gives life and perspective to the Good News we believe and teach. There is a remarkable phrase found in the Acts of the Apostles. The disciples have gathered to choose someone to replace Judas who killed himself. Peter calls the disciples together and explains in these words the task at hand:

> We must therefore choose someone who has been with us the whole time that the Lord Jesus was traveling round with us, someone who was with us right from the time when John was baptizing until the day when he was taken up from us—and he can act with us as a witness to his resurrection (Acts 1:21-22).

This is the definition of an apostle: a witness to the resurrection. When we do not witness to the resurrection whatever our labor and our service, we are not apostles. On the other hand, when we radiate the joy and faith of the risen Lord we are real apostles, whatever we do. The heart of the apostolate

167

is the witness to the resurrection. All the rest is secondary.

Teilhard de Chardin complains in a letter that we Christians are no longer contagious. Our religion has become dull, mediocre, perhaps because the faith in the resurrection is no longer the focus. The resurrection meant everything to the early Christians. Perhaps we have repressed it. Other things are more important to us. Then our faith is dull indeed. It is notable how quickly the membership of the early Church grew because the disciples had that unity in faith and that witnessing power which attracted people.

Why is the resurrection so important, so central to our faith? The resurrection is "not information about another world we have not traveled; the resurrection is divine self-revelation" (Gregory Baum). God shows himself as he really is in the resurrection. It reveals to us the clearest insight we have into the being of God. The more we know God, the more we know of our own lives, too. It is divine self-revelation, and, therefore, an x-raying of our own existence as well: "Eternal life is this: to know you the only true God and Jesus Christ whom you have sent" (Jn 17:3). When we know God better, when God reveals himself, our own lives receive more depth, more substance.

The resurrection is the best way to know who God is because it gives dimension to the love which God is. We believe in the love which God has for us, and in the resurrection we can see that the love of God for us has no limits. It is not that God loves us for a lifetime. He loves us and he wants us to live forever. That is the reliability of God's love. When we speak of God's love without believing in the resurrection, we are dealing with a projection. Love of God for a lifetime is a human creation, the projection of a petty, narrow-minded human heart which craves some affection. There is nothing divine in this. The Gospel says we are loved by God, and the love of God doesn't end in death. It goes beyond it. Death is no hindrance to the love of God. In Luke (Chapter 20) Christ is attacked by the Sadducees about the resurrection of the dead. What is going to happen to the woman who claims seven husbands? Christ dismisses the humorous example and points to the essence: the reliability of God's love. The resurrection shows the limitlessness of God's reliability. "Strong as death is love" says the Song of Songs (8:6) but the resurrection proves that God's love is stronger than death. Now we are secure and safe in the love of God. Now we know that there is no limit to it. His forgiveness makes evident that our sins are drowned in his love. The resurrection reveals that our death is overcome by his love. Now we can really trust God and rely on him. All fear will disappear from our lives. The resurrection unearths the depth, the quality of the reliability of God's love. Psalm 118 is a real Easter psalm: "Give thanks to Yahweh for he is good; his love is everlasting." This is what we have to assure one another. But we can only do so if we believe in the resurrection. Otherwise, we do not believe that his love is everlasting:

Hard-pressed, I invoked Yahweh,
he heard me and came to my relief.

AS BREAD THAT IS BROKEN

With Yahweh on my side, I fear nothing:
What can man do to me?
With Yahweh on my side, best help of all,
I can triumph over my enemies.

I was pressed, pressed, about to fall,
but Yahweh came to my help;
Yahweh is my strength and my song,
he has been my saviour.

No, I shall not die, I shall live
to recite the deeds of Yahweh;

It was the stone rejected by the builders
that proved to be the keystone;
this is Yahweh's doing
and it is wonderful to see.
This is the day made memorable by Yahweh,
what immense joy for us!

Give thanks to Yahweh, for he is good,
his love is everlasting! (Ps 118:5-7,13-14,17,22-24,29).

We believe not in an abstract god but in the God who
is the Father of our Lord Jesus Christ. The Father of
whom Jesus always spoke—that's the God we believe
in. Above all, the Father who raised Jesus from the
dead—that is the God we believe in: "Our faith too
will be 'considered' if we believe in him who raised
Jesus our Lord from the dead" (Rom 4:24). That
same Father of our Lord Jesus Christ is interested in
each one of us and loves each one of us. That same
divine love is spent on us. The risen Lord knows us.
His love and interest goes out to each of us.

Twenty

THE BEST OF ALL GOOD THINGS

The Holy Spirit is the fullness of what God has to give. In liturgy there is a host of images and comparisons to express what the Holy Spirit does and is. He sanctifies, he strengthens, he consoles. He warms when we are chilly, he helps, he cures and heals. He makes supple what has become stiff, he cleanses, he enlightens when it is dark. He is a tongue, a dove. He is fire, storm, light and dew. He is breath. He is the finger of God with which God made the universe. He constantly renews the face of the earth.

In his farewell discourse, Christ speaks much about the Holy Spirit. He says that it is better for us that he leaves: "Still, I must tell you the truth: it is for your own good that I am going because unless I go, the Advocate will not come to you; but if I do go, I will send him to you" (Jn 16:7). The gift of the Spirit is more precious than the presence of Christ himself. In that Spirit Christ is closer to us. He is right in the midst of our being. The Spirit is the fullness of what Christ can give: "The Advocate, the Holy Spirit, whom the Father will send in my name, will teach you everything and remind you of all I have said to you" (Jn 14:26). Everything and all the Word contains in its integrity is brought home to us in the literal sense—brought right into our hearts.

171

The great biblical theme of the living water had its liturgical celebration on the last day of the feast of tabernacles when the temple square would be overflowing with people. In the midst of that liturgy Jesus cried out to the crowd: "If any man is thirsty, let him come to me!" These people celebrated but they did not know what they were celebrating. They did not realize the meaning of their own symbols. The true source of living water is not the well of Siloam where the priests drew water but Christ himself. "Let the man come and drink who believes in me!" As scripture says: "From his breast shall flow fountains of living water." And for those who did not understand the symbolism, John added, "He was speaking of the Spirit which those who believed in him were to receive; for there was no Spirit as yet because Jesus had not yet been glorified" (Jn 7:37-39). The Spirit can only be given after the glorification of Christ. We can say that the life of Christ terminates with the crucifixion. That is the sad conclusion of Jesus' life. But the cross is not the last word. The cross turns into the glorification of the resurrection which will last forever. But for us there is a sequence to the glory of the resurrection, namely, the gift of the Holy Spirit. Only when Christ has completed everything—life, death, resurrection, return to the Father—can he give us his Holy Spirit. Christ lived for this one purpose—to achieve for us this gift: "I was born for this, I came into the world for this: to bear witness to the truth" (Jn 18:37). And *the* witness to God's truth is the Holy Spirit himself. To bring the Truth into this world is the fullness, the apotheosis of the whole existence of Christ.

Who is the Holy Spirit? This is a difficult question to answer. Anthony Bloom relates this tale: "A Japanese once said to me: 'In the Christian religion I think I understand about the Father and the Son, but I can never discover the significance of the honorable bird.' "[1] For many Christians, too, this "honorable bird" is the great unknown. He was so in the early Church: "When Paul asked, 'Did you receive the Holy Spirit when you became believers?' they answered, 'No, we were never even told there was such a thing as a Holy Spirit' " (Acts 19:2). For many present-day Christians the situation is only slightly better. Who is the Holy Spirit? If this is *the* gift of God, we should at least try to grasp a little of the mystery.

* * * *

The Holy Spirit is the third Person of the Blessed Trinity. This simple statement says a great deal. It means that God is a "family." God is not a lonely God. He is not the "unmoved all-mover" of Aristotle nor the Narcissus of the philosophers, a God who is only interested in himself. But God is community. God is life together. In God there is begetting and knowing and loving. In God there is perfect communication. The Father's whole self is expressed in the Word which is the Son. And the Son surrenders himself to his Father in complete abandonment without holding anything back. The two open themselves up totally. Loneliness in human life is a great pain. God has the bliss of being together: I and Thou, Father and Son, who can look one another in the face. But then in our human lives when we are together, there is always that shadow of division, a rift which we cannot mend. We can never reach the other person as completely as we would like. There is always the mystery, something which we cannot understand about the other person. There is always the helplessness of separation. That division is not in God. In God there is a togetherness which is complete, which has no shadow. It is the sharing of one single life. It is the knowledge of the other person in an unbroken unity. And it is the Holy Spirit who is that miracle—two persons who live one life. The Holy Spirit is the bond of perfect unity between Father and Son.

For us human beings love is a power which achieves the incredible. Love is the greatest force on earth. But with God love is more than something. With God love is someone, a person. And that is the Third Person of the Blessed Trinity. He is the miraculous love who unites the Father and the Son into a perfect unity. He is that bond of openness of the Father to the Son and the Son to the Father. He is the reality that really counts: God's love which is based on nothing. He is the ultimate foundation. He is the heart of all being. That same love is given to us: "The love of God has been poured into our hearts by the Holy Spirit which has been given us" (Rom 5:5). The deepest of all mysteries has been given to us in the Holy Spirit who is God's love in Person. To a certain extent he works that same miracle among men. There again he creates community. When the apostles were expecting the Holy Spirit they were united in a continuous and unanimous prayer. That

174

was a foreshadowing of his coming. And when he really came on the feast of Pentecost, he worked a tremendous miracle in them. They all of a sudden understood each other's language. People who had been separated came closer, understood what the other meant. That is the miracle of the Holy Spirit. He is never just a gift given personally but is always meant to create community, to bring persons together. He unites those to whom he is given, and thus forms the Church, the community of the Holy Spirit. The Holy Spirit is the love of God which Jesus has communicated to us, to which he witnessed and which he brought into this world and which has to continue through us. The Holy Spirit is that love of God which is the completion of everything: "faith, hope and charity—there remain these three: but the greatest of these is charity" (1 Cor 13:13). That is the Holy Spirit.

* * * *

A second reply to the question "Who is the Holy Spirit?" identifies the Holy Spirit as the Spirit of Christ, the mind, the mentality of Christ:

> I shall ask the Father, and he will give you another Advocate to be with you forever, that Spirit of truth whom the world can never receive since it neither sees nor knows him; but you know him, because he is with you, he is in you. I will not leave you orphans; I will come back to you (Jn 14:16-18).

In his Spirit Christ is with us: "When the Advocate comes, whom I shall send to you from the Father, the Spirit of truth who issues from the

Father, he will be my witness" (Jn 15:26). When are two people together? Not when their bodies touch. That is not enough. Judas was not close to Jesus when he kissed him in the garden of Gethsemane. Only when the minds of two persons are one are they present to each other. So, too, is Christ with us through and in his Spirit: "In fact, unless you possessed the Spirit of Christ you would not belong to him" (Rom 8:9). Only in that Spirit are we Christians: "But we are those who have the mind of Christ" (1 Cor 2:16).

To have the mind of Christ means that we actually begin to think as Christ thinks and to feel as Christ feels. His mind, his attitudes animate us. There is only one way to the Father and that is through Christ. There is only one way to Christ and that is through his Spirit. The Holy Spirit is at once the completion of Christ's mission on earth and the inception of our life as Christians. There are three vital dimensions of our life which, if open to the influence of the Holy Spirit, reflect this transformation.

It is the Spirit of Christ which teaches us our concept of God:

> Everyone moved by the Spirit is a son of God. The spirit you received is not the spirit of slaves bringing fear into your lives again; it is the spirit of sons, and it makes us cry out, 'Abba, Father' " (Rom 8:14).

The paralyzing fear of God is taken out of our hearts. We call God "Abba" as Christ did in the perfect security of his sonship. When we are totally filled with the Spirit, nothing upsets us in our prayer.

Without any effort, without any strain we surrender. Rooted in the conviction that God is love and the source of life, we find no evil, no threat in his presence. As for Christ so also for us the will of God is the obvious work to be accomplished and the nourishment on which we live. The more the Spirit is given to us, the more this type of relation with God will grow.

The Spirit of Christ affects not only our relationship with God but also with other people. Christ had respect for everybody. His delicate and open response to each person he met along the way endorsed the brotherhood of man. All are children of the Father: his Father and their Father. He could and did accept everybody. In and through this Spirit of Christ we, too, are enabled to accept whoever comes our way with real respect which is the heart of love.

The Spirit of Christ touches our relationship to things. Christ lived in the spirit of truth and that made him free. It is this interior freedom which gives us the ability to use this world's goods without becoming enslaved by them. St. Francis of Assisi enjoyed the things of this world immensely because he did not possess them. He was completely free. When we are attached to things, we worry about them. When we do not cling to anything, we do not have to worry: Seek first the kingdom of God and the rest will be given to you (Lk 12:31). Christ did not think it was necessary to possess anything, and the Father indeed took good care of him!

The Spirit too comes to help us in our weakness. For when we cannot choose words in order to pray properly,

177

the Spirit himself expresses our plea in a way that could never be put into words (Rom 8:26).

The Spirit himself prays in us. Prayer becomes so simple. More and more we learn to listen to Jesus who prays in us. The desert Fathers described Christian prayer as listening deeply within ourselves to the prayer Jesus utters through his Spirit to his Father. In this sense our prayer becomes more passive. We are not doing the praying, but the Spirit, or Jesus himself, prays in us.

The Holy Spirit is the mind of Christ which takes hold of us: "No one can say 'Jesus is Lord' unless he is under the influence of the Holy Spirit" (1 Cor 12:3). This unadorned formula, so brief, so easy to pronounce, is the most difficult prayer in the world. To pray "Jesus is Lord" means an unreserved giving of ourselves to Christ. He is Lord. He may tell us what to do. To pray "Jesus is Lord" is to acknowledge Christ as Lord of the universe. Everything in this world is less important, less powerful than he. Only the Spirit enables us to pray this prayer.

* * * *

The third answer to the question "Who is the Holy Spirit?" is found by asking what does the Spirit accomplish? From what activities can his presence in our lives be discerned? The Holy Spirit makes us witnesses to the very ends of the earth (Acts 1:8). Like Christ himself, we witness to the truth which is the faithfulness of God's love. And we can bear

178

witness to it to the extent that we ourselves are full of the Spirit, that Christ is our life—the core of our existence. To convey the various levels of truth, wisdom and knowledge demands a variety of approaches. For instance, if we are trying to convey mathematical truth to a class of students, we have to be patient, precise in our choice of terminology, slow to proceed from step-to-step. If we are involved in transmitting psychological truth, for example, in counseling, we employ a far different technique. Then directly or indirectly, we try to make the person realize, recognize and feel in himself what is being said so that he can relate his own experience to what he hears as true. Again, the imparting of religious truth necessitates another approach. Here the only valid mode of operation is the personal witness of the one who speaks—the parent, the teacher, the priest or religious, the friend, the man of the street. Teaching, proving, demonstrating, arguing will not satisfy. In fact, the one who witnesses to religious truth will concentrate on less arguing and more witnessing, less discussion and more sharing, less intellectualism and more Holy Spirit. To witness is far more demanding than all the intellectualism our brains can produce:

> Witnessing involves not only the competence and the knowledge of the one who attests but it involves him or her as a person and that's much more. We conclude then that testimony, witnessing, is not mere communications. It involves the dynamic power of the Holy Spirit carrying with it full conviction: 'When we brought the Good News to you, it came to you not only as words, but as power and as the Holy Spirit and as utter conviction.'[2]

When we are imbued with the complete truth which is Spirit, then we can witness: "But when the Spirit of truth comes he will lead you to the complete truth" (Jn 16:13). It takes courage to speak the truth that is Spirit to others. Mere intellectualism is far easier because it is safe! We cannot be wounded. A witness makes himself vulnerable. He puts not only his brains but also his heart at stake. To witness means to be defenseless. It hurts when our witnessing (and that means *we*) is not accepted. There is no apostolate without the willingness to suffer that sort of pain. We can hide behind brilliant arguments and we won't be hurt. But we won't be heard, either.

Religious life should be a witnessing. This is to say that we do not have a defense to offer those who judge religious life, contest it, who wish to renovate it without themselves possessing an integral faith and a supernatural hope. Outsiders or religious themselves can eas - ily make many complaints against religious life. They may be correct in what they say and yet be missing the right spirit, the Holy Spirit, the real integration. To witness to religious life means that the life in itself has value for us and gives us fulfillment. We do not live it to convince others. That is not witness. That is a facade. To witness in religious life means that even if others do not understand or approve we are full of hope. This is basic to witnessing: who loses his soul will find it. Witnessing is unselfish, disinterested. The Holy Spirit makes us into witnesses. The fruits of the Spirit shape the type of person who is a true witness to Christ even in the midst of pain and hardships: "What the Spirit brings is...love, joy, peace, patience, kindness, goodness, trustfulness, gentleness, and self-control" (Gal 5:22).

A Penance Service

"With you, O Lord, there is forgiveness and on this we live."

All sing: Entrance Song "Yes I Shall Arise" (Lucien Deiss)

Celebrant: Introduction
The grace and peace of God our Father and of our Lord Jesus Christ be with you.

We have come together as sinful people who want to admit that we are so. The common confession of that sinfulness and the communal experience of God's forgiveness can bring us closer together as a community. It can also deepen our conscience and open our eyes to what we would not see perhaps by ourselves. These are the advantages of a penance service over a private confession. The personal confession has its special value, too, mainly that I express explicitly in words spoken aloud to someone else my concrete sins and receive the personal sacramental absolution. Thus I commit myself and, in a human way, absorb God's forgiveness. So the penance service and the private confession have their own special merits. They should not exclude but complement each other. The check on a good penance service is a more pertinent personal confession; and the check on a good private confession is a more intense celebration of the penance service.

Celebrant: Opening Prayer
God our Father, let us not seek false names to cover

up our sins, and let us not try to escape the gift of your forgiveness. You never fail any one of your people. Your greatest joy is to exercise your forgiveness in accepting one who went astray, who was lost and came back home. We come today to let ourselves be forgiven. We approach you without any rights, but we are certain that you come to meet us with open arms and a deep joy because you are our Father, today, and everyday, forever and ever.

All: Amen.

Lector: Old Testament Reading, Isaiah 52:14-53:6 or 2 Cor 5:17-21

All: Responsorial Psalm — Psalm 130

Antiphon: "To you I lift up my heart; in you I place my trust."

Lector: New Testament Reading — Lk 15:11-24 or Lk 7:36-50

Litany of Petitions
Let us pray to God who is our Father that he may give us the grace of true contrition. . .Let us pray to the Lord. *Response:* Lord, hear our prayer.
That we may have the courage to face our life and to judge it. . .
That he may keep us from scrupulousness and from shallowness. . .
That he may keep us from despair and from lack of contrition. . .

182

That we may not restrict ourselves to the disappointments in our own selves and to the dents in our own excellence, but that we may also touch your love from which we shielded ourselves and you whom we've hurt. . .

That the hard light of truth may unveil to us the reality of our lives and that courageously we may endure the pain of this unveiling, and that God's love for us as we are may always be the deepest foundation of this whole celebration. . .

That we may believe in the love of you, our Father, and may be secure in that love, and that we may deep down in our hearts experience your grace and your kindness. . .

That we may inspire each other to a more authentic repentance, and that you may be in our midst since we are gathered in your name. . .

Forgive us, Lord, that we were too little our own selves, that likes and dislikes were sometimes more important to us than our own conscience; that we did not seek the deepest Ground of our existence but stayed somewhere on the surface; that we did not try to discover your guidance in our lives, and that we hurt your holy will; that sometimes we did not even provide for a climate of interior stillness in which alone your voice can be heard; that we did not shine forth peace and joy but restlessness and discontent. . .

Forgive us, Lord, that we sometimes too easily dismissed our prayer and excused ourselves when it was not necessary at all, and sometimes didn't make an effort to be really still in your presence; forgive us, Lord, for the time which we wasted in laziness, for the distractions which we welcomed, for the dozing, and for the times we appeared before you only partly prepared. . .

Forgive us, Lord, that sometimes we have been lazy—too lazy to get up, too slow to help—that we did not accept inconveniences or changes in plans graciously; that we delayed unpleasant plans and tasks, and sometimes delayed them so long that they could not be done anymore; that our conversation was sometimes shallow; that we didn't really search for the depth in our lives. . .

Forgive us, Lord, for all our unworthy thoughts, our judgments of others, our unfair criticism and our inner discontent; the sensual fantasies which we fostered, moodiness and despondency which we nourished. . .

Forgive us, Lord, for failing to turn to you in our moments of loneliness. . .

Forgive us, Lord, for our reckless speech, the harshness of our words, the rashness of our opinions, the lies and half truths that we uttered. . .

Forgive us, Lord, for what we have not said when the situation demanded it. . .

Forgive us, Lord, that sometimes we have been factious; that we sowed divisions in our community; that sometimes we have put people at odds with one another by tattling; that we stirred up suspicion; that we undermined trust among men and among the members of our community; that through our guilt our community is less one that you expect; that perhaps through our rigidity or laxity, we are partly guilty that some have left the community. . .

Forgive us, Lord, that sometimes we have been conceited; that we tried to make ourselves important, to dominate, to build up our own image; that sometimes we were not really sincere and tried to create a semblance to which no reality corresponds; that we've tried to make ourselves popular; that we wanted to be right in front and with it. . .

Forgive us, Lord, that sometimes we showed little enthusiasm in our faith; that through a cultivated mediocrity we did not do justice to the true face of Christ and the true meaning of the Gospel in the eyes of our fellow men; that we have been unfaithful in our mission; that sometimes through selfishness we tried to include in our vocation what does not agree with it. . .

Forgive us, Lord, if sometimes we lived in too great a luxury; if we closed our hearts to the needs of this world; if we abused the movement of renewal in the Church to make ourselves richer and to improve our standard of living; that we placed our needs and desires above those of the community; that we used unfair diplomacy to advance our own desires; that we tried to dominate instead of to serve. . .

(For those who live a celibate life) Forgive us, Lord, that sometimes we did not try to live the fullness of celibacy; that we did not try to let the love of Christ fill our hearts and lives; that we looked for substitutes and compensations thus depriving the people committed to our care of the deeper inspiration celibacy is meant to be for them. . .

Forgive us, Lord, that sometimes we opened ourselves too little to the deeper intention of the other and to the deeper meaning of God's spirit in our time. . .

Forgive us, Lord, when we were slow and tepid and lived more according to the letter than to the spirit; when we tried to leave things as they are and did not have the courage to begin anew. . .

Forgive us, Lord, our faults of omission: the help we could have given, the comfort which was expected from us, the sorrow we did not even see, the inspiration which we denied others, your longing for us which we did not want to hear. . .

Celebrant: Prayer

O God, I come to you as a member of this community, admitting my own weakness and sins and asking for forgiveness. I am sorry for the many times that I have turned away from you to my shallow, untrue self and have taken away from the full strength and stature the Body of Christ could have in our community. Each of my infidelities has done harm to others, not showing the real depth of what the Gospel should mean for them.

Silent Reflection

All: Psalm 51 (as a common confession)

186

A Penance Service

Celebrant: Concluding Prayer
May almighty God have mercy on us, forgive us our sins, and bring us to everlasting life.

All: Amen.

Celebrant: May the almighty and merciful God grant us pardon, absolution and remission of our sins.

All: Amen.

Celebrant: Almighty God will have mercy on us because of his Son, Jesus Christ, who surrendered himself for us and carries all our sins. The power, the kingdom and the glory are his. May he bless us and keep us, may his face shine upon us and may he give us peace and grace today and every day, forever and ever.

All: Amen.

Celebrant: May the passion of our Lord Jesus Christ, the merits of the Blessed Virgin Mary and of all the saints, whatever good we have done and evil we have endured, achieve for us the forgiveness of our sins, the increase of grace and the reward of everlasting life.

All: Amen.

All sing: recessional "Grant To Us, O Lord" (Lucien Deiss)

FOOTNOTES

Unless otherwise stated all biblical quotations are taken from *The Jerusalem Bible* (New York: Doubleday & Company, Inc., 1966). The abbreviation NAB refers to *The New American Bible,* St. Joseph Edition (New York: Catholic Book Publishing Company, 1970).

Chapter One

[1](New York: W. W. Norton & Co., 1958), 118.

Chapter Two

[1]*A New Catechism: Catholic Faith for Adults,* trans. Kevin Smyth (New York: Herder and Herder, 1967), 382.

[2]*The Confessions,* Book X, Chapter 27.

[3]Huub Oosterhuis et al, *Fifty Psalms: An Attempt at a New Translation* (New York: Herder and Herder, 1969), 74.

[4]Dietrich Bonhoeffer, *Letters and Papers from Prison* edit. by Eberhard Bethge, rev. ed. (New York: The Macmillan Company, 1967), 155.

[5]Paul Tillich, *The Courage To Be* (New Haven: Yale University Press, 1952), 187.

Chapter Four

[1](Denville: Dimension Books, Inc., 1973), 18.

[2]Quoted by Farrell, *op. cit.,* 114.

[3]Dietrich Bonhoeffer, *op. cit.,* 213-14.

[4]Martin Buber, *I and Thou* trans. Ronald Gregor Smith (New York: Charles Scribner's Sons, 1937),9.

[5]*Contemplative Prayer,* (New York: Herder and Herder, 1969), 135.

Chapter Five

[1]Perry D. Lefevre, *The Prayers of Kierkegaard* (Chicago, The University of Chicago Press, 1969[4]), 14

[2]Thomas Merton, *op. cit.,* 113.

Chapter Seven

[1]Much of this thought is taken from *Jacques Guillet, The Consciousness of Jesus* (New Jersey: Paulist/Newman Press, 1972), 63-5.

[2]I owe these thoughts to W. H. van de Pol, *Het Voortbestaan van Kerk en Christendom* (Roermond, 1969).

[3]David M. Stanley, S.J., *Faith and Religious Life* (New Jersey: Paulist/Newman Press, 1971), 14.

[4]This text is the highlight of Mark's Gospel. Mk 1:1 begins by saying: "The beginning of the Good News about Jesus Christ, the Son of God." Mk 8:29 is the first peak of this message when Jesus is called "Christ" by Peter. Mk 15:39 is the ultimate peak when Jesus is called "Son of God" by the centurion.

Chapter Eight

[1]Edward Farrell, *Prayer is a Hunger* (Denville: Dimension Books, Inc., 1972), 50.

Chapter Nine

[1]A. F. Wyers, "Het Tweegesprek Met God," *De Bazuin,* August 15, 1959.

Chapter Ten

[1]We still find the baptism of Christ recorded in the first chapter of Mark's Gospel. Both Luke and Matthew record the

event in the third chapter only because the first and second chapters were added at a later date. John follows the same order of Matthew and Luke but expressed in his own way.

Chapter Eleven

[1] Huub Oosterhuis et al, *op. cit.,* 29.

[2] Ibid., 84.

Chapter Twelve

[1] Martin Buber, *op. cit.,* 52.

[2] Carlo Carretto, *Letters from the Desert* (Maryknoll: Orbis Books, 1972), 81.

[3] Edward Farrell, *Surprised by the Spirit,* 38.

Chapter Thirteen

[1] Rene Voillaume, Conferences to Religious Superiors, 1970. Unpublished manuscript.

[2] David M. Stanley, *op. cit.,* 82.

Chapter Fourteen

[1] Paul Tillich, *Love, Power and Justice* (London: Oxford University Press, 1960), 119.

Chapter Fifteen

[1] Ladislaus Boros, *God Is With Us* (New York: Herder and Herder, 1967), 170.
[2] Ibid.,

[3]Ladislaus Boros, *We Are Future* (New York: Herder and Herder, 1960). 74.

Chapter Sixteen

[1]Romano Guardini, *The Lord* (Chicago: Henry Regnery Company, 1954), 244-47.

[2]Anthony Padovano, *Dawn Without Darkness* (New Jersey: Paulist/Newman Press, 1971), 15.

[3]Anthony Bloom, *Living Prayer* (Springfield; Illinois: Templegate Publishers, 1971), 98.

[4]Dietrich Bonhoeffer, *op. cit.,* 188.

Chapter Twenty

[1]Anthony Bloom, *Meditations: A Spiritual Journey* (Denville: Dimension Books, Inc. 1972), 26.

[2]David M. Stanley, *op. cit.,* 6-7.